D1644571

Enlivened
by the
Mystery

Quakers and God

Friends Bulletin

Edited by Kathy Hyzy

Published by Friends Bulletin Corporation
United States of America
Friends Bulletin Corporation is the publisher of *Western Friend*, the
official publication of Pacific, North Pacific, and Intermountain Yearly
Meetings of the Religious Society of Friends.
Opinions expressed in this book are of the authors, not necessarily of
the Yearly Meetings.

First printing November 2009

Cover design by Meredith Jacobson
Sight&Sense, www.sightandsense.com

Cover art: "Shot Through"
 by Cherrill Boissonou

Table of Contents

Storytelling, particularly from our own experiences, is at the heart of Quakerism. Read the journals of early Friends like Margaret Fell or John Woolman, and you find they frequently write passionately and at length about their mystical experiences. Ministry on First Day is likely to include Friends sharing anecdotes from their own lives—sometimes to illustrate a point, sometimes witnessing to a direct experience of the Divine in their ordinary lives.

While for many years Friends turned away from artistic forms to tell their stories, today they are an essential part of how we share the gifts of the Spirit. These forms express different ways of knowing beauty and wonder, and make them accessible to others in a way that plain telling cannot. Sometimes a picture is worth a thousand words of praise, and a poem is the only way to truly witness to the ineffable mystery we have experienced. And sometimes the process of attempting to capture the mystery is an act of prayer in and of itself.

Enlivened by the Mystery is an effort to celebrate these other ways of encountering and expressing the Divine. We hope it is the first of several books in a series titled *Giving Form to Faith*, which will continue to employ creative arts to explore other topics of importance to Friends. The series is particularly interested in lifting up the voices of Quakers in the West, who are often far from one another and far from the centers of U.S. Quakerism.

Creating this book was a leap of faith, relying upon the readers of *Western Friend* magazine to take to heart an invitation to share their stories. Several queries accompanied that invitation, but the primary one was simply, "How have you experienced God or the Divine?"

And what a gift in the response! We could not include every story, poem, or photo, but I do believe the pieces here represent that enlivening Spirit which moves us all. The shape of the book arose from those responses. The themed sections echo sections common to a Faith & Practice, but also reflect the natural affinities between the pieces chosen for the anthology. And the title (always a challenge!) surfaced while reading a piece written by San Fransisco Friend cubbie storm, which is included here.

How to Read this Book

This book is meant to be accessible to Friends no matter how busy their lives. It can be used as a devotional, reading a piece or two a day, or simply read cover to cover. Friends who are interested in guided worship sharing may find the brief queries at the beginning of each section to be helpful.

Anthologies often strive to group similar-sounding and complimentary voices with one another. You won't find that approach in these pages. Sometimes it does occur, but you are just as likely to find contrasts as you move from pages to page in a given section. Quakers, particularly in the West, come at the world from a plethora of angles, and this anthology seeks to honor that diversity.

If you *do* choose to read this collection from cover to cover, please consider taking it slow, allowing time for the words and images to seep in before moving to the next. As I have spent time with these pieces over the past few months, I have been surprised at the new insights and wisdom I find even today.

Acknowledgements

I am so very grateful to all the Friends who responded to the nudge and sent in their stories, poetry, and artwork. You are ministering to the wider Quaker community, and you have ministered to—and enlivened—me throughout the process of creating this book. Heartfelt thanks also goes to the Board of Friends Bulletin Corporation, without whose patience, vision and hands-on support this book would not exist.

In the Light,

Kathy Hyzy
Editor

MYSTERY

QUERIES

Does seeking to name or articulate your experience of Mystery bring greater clarity or deeper understanding?

What are the ways that experiencing The Mystery brings changes to your faith and daily life?

How have you been a part of nurturing this sense of awe and mystery in others?

INTO THE HEART OF MYSTERY

Connie Fledderjohann

FUSION

Clots of cream and dung became new worlds of birds and tongues
transformed by time, and beating hearts and pleas of spirits rising
seaweed, snails and mysteries
and mackerel and old bees dead beyond all buzzing

Transformed by time, and beating hearts and pleas of spirits rising
I walked and flew
and mackerel and old bees dead beyond all buzzing
all walked and flew

I walked and flew
and whales, and time and water bugs
all walked and flew
into my soul

And whales, and time and water bugs
worked their way
into my soul
and were me and I, they

Worked their way
with my soul
and were me and I, they
until we all were one

With my soul
clots of cream and dung became new worlds of birds and tongues
until we all were one –
seaweed, snails and mysteries.

Helen Bruner

4

FERMENTATION

When the growing season ends, we make sauerkraut.
Mom shreds the cabbage, knife rasping against
tightly layered leaves. Then she adds salt and whey,
pounds everything until it bruises and weeps, and
shoves the limp cabbage into a quart jar.
She screws the lid on tight.

Every now and then, I go to the basement and
check on the sauerkraut. I peer through the glass
jar and see little bubbles. Sometimes they rise to
the surface as I watch. The brine seeps out
beneath the lid and trickles down the sides,
pooling on the floor. Inside, the cabbage
is steeping, changing, becoming.

New wine, Jesus said, and surely he knew
about dark, cool silence, the sour smell
of ripening. But he also knew how life breaks
the seal and comes bursting out one morning,
green and pungent, fresh with salty
tang on its lips.

Eileen R. Kinch

RIVEN BY LIGHT

Rivers far away are arcing over rocks, falling
in foaming swirls, plunging, light as rain:
flying water, momentary and endless
at once, like a storm seen from a distance—
movement that seems still.
The world wakes continually, is riven
by beginnings, ferns fiercely
unfurling through duff, sunlight
like countless fine hands reaching in through
cracks in the soil to find the word,
the seed, the name, the forgotten thing
waiting to be warmed.

Tina Tau

JUST SITTING THERE

"Don't just do something...sit there!" - A Quaker expression

harvest moon
entering the dark temple
i bow to shadows

in silence
awaiting the teacher's bell
windchimes

meditating-
our shadows on the floor
pass so quickly...

a parked car
racing its engine; an incense stick
drops ash

chips scatter!
he whacks away at his still
unfinished Buddha

Anthony Manousos

BETWEEN THE INNER PLACES

Do not seek the Beloved
In devotion
Flung out to the Power
Encompassing.

Seek it rather
In the Awe
Of the inner places
Between the cells of Being
Attention breathing there
Uncovers
All the Light that Is.

Maria Arrington

BREAK IN THE MAIN LINE

Thirsty and tenacious, roots
invade the drainage system
and laundry water backs up into
the bathtub. Will the young apricot tree
have to be moved, and Heavenly Bamboo?
Is the old rhododendron responsible?

A broken pipe changes the landscape,
says it's all one life, open or closed
it's all one, *subterra* busy
with noise, forgotten connections
rushing to the surface.

Little by little, the roots
push out of confinement
tangled balls that give way
to rotating knives and the snake,
the plumber's sweat.

Nothing stops the hidden life.
Live long enough and you learn
to take heed of your own,
relinquish what you love:
sweet apricot flesh,
shining scarlet berries.

Jeanne Lohmann

DRIVING TO THE COLD HOLLOW MOUNTAINS

for Geoff Hewitt

Strayed on the wide roads that drive north into Canada,
I've been drummed all day into the pitched colors
of the leaves dying. Times over, many times,
I found my hand a hard fist on the steering wheel
and my throat harsh with swallowing salt
in my laughter, love scraping the soaked air
for the trees
that declare their own bright translation
to the white houses and the weathered barns
they've lived next to all year.

For God's seal is on the trees:
They're going crazy in crowds by immovable boulders
and huge wet outcrops of granite,
or going crazy alone in certain patches of land
stretched fallow beside the black highways.
They go staggering, headlong exaltations of light,
as if God were asking in the red leaves
that shatter with visible rage the flared blue sky:
Where wast thou when I laid the foundations of the earth?

I grant I was not here,
that I have no understanding of these changes.
Things happen.
I don't ask for answers any more,
but I have not learned how to suffer without noise
anything
even illuminations of dead leaves.

Nevertheless, if this is how things fall apart
then let the Last Day come
beating on the ruddy hillsides,
bearing God's seal to hurt not the trees,
His last seal
which is silence.

Phyllis Hoge

CARRIED ON BY LOVE

When I don't know where to be/ I let Your memory move in me
Like a wave upon the sea/ I'm carried on by love

-Clare Norelle

Most of the time it's in little ways that the Divine breaks through to me, brings comfort, challenge, healing and Grace into my life. But once in a while I'm washed over, lifted up and turned around. Sometimes when nudging and whispering don't work, it takes a clap of thunder or a jolt of reawakening to get the message across. Often it's a simple message that I've heard a zillion times before, but drawn larger or in a deeper hue. Last September it took something more vivid to get the message through to me.

For several years I have been studying Reiki, a Japanese practice of energy work that reduces stress, relaxes and can promote healing. On a Reiki retreat at the coast, I was trying to leave behind new meeting responsibilities—yet I was concerned about people in meeting, as well as family and friends. I wanted to figure out what else I could or should do to help in various situations. At the same time, I was trying to be present for the experiences we were sharing during the weekend.

The last morning after a movement meditation on the beach, I knew that I needed to let go and just be present. I asked for a Reiki treatment and lay down on the living room floor. A wave of sadness broke over me, and the darkness and difficulties of the world seemed immense. Sobs escaped me. As others kneeled down and laid their gentle hands upon me, I let the tension rock my soul.

Time wasn't a factor now, but I was aware of others in the room hearing my cries and turning loving attention my way. Then, I felt lifted up and carried out beyond the shore over the shining waves to the middle of the Pacific Ocean. I remember thinking that it was like being transported on an air mattress, or as the psalmist put it being held by the Everlasting Arms. Later I wrote,

Floated out over the ocean on loving hands
Buoyant with the Universal Energy of Light.

I had been there before. Thirty years earlier on a small sailboat with my husband, our nine month old baby and a friend we had been on

11

this silver blue grey vastness crossing over three thousand miles of sea to Hawaii.

Now it lay out underneath me.

Then the words came clearly, "You silly girl! Didn't I hold you across this ocean before? Surely I am holding you now!"

Of course. When the baby's fever passed, the gale subsided and we came to safe harbor after a month at sea, I said I would never forget. How could I ever forget that moment-by-moment experience of God's Presence?

Well, it's easy, I've discovered.

I began laughing. What on earth was there to fear now compared to *that*? There I was doubting, worrying and trying to do it all on my own again.

Then another message came clearly, as if someone else was right along side me out there. "Everyone is already loved in a whole and perfect way."

Oh thank God! It wasn't up to me.

God's Love and Presence, that perfect Source of Life, reaches out to everyone all the time. It's my responsibility to live out my own light and seek what Love would have me do in joy and patience. But then, in prayer and gratitude, I am to release those I worry about to God's care and bless them on their path.

What a relief! I can do that. Gently, I was brought back to the room and the friends that had been ministering to me.

Some months later, in the early morning, as this time of Grace vividly replayed in my mind, a P.S. was added to the message.

"Just remind them."

So that is part of my calling now. Let us notice all the ways the Creator is active in our lives. Let us give thanks for the small nudges and whispers as well as for the jolts, healings and dramatic turnarounds. You are already loved in a whole and perfect way. What an amazing assurance! Even when we personally fall short, as we will, we can know that we are loved.

We can step out on that Grace and be carried on by Love.

Betsey Kenworthy

GOD

QUERIES

What practices have you found that encourage your attentiveness to the Holy Spirit?

Do you honor the leadings of the Inward Teacher, even when they place great demands on you?

How has your understanding or perception of God changed over time?

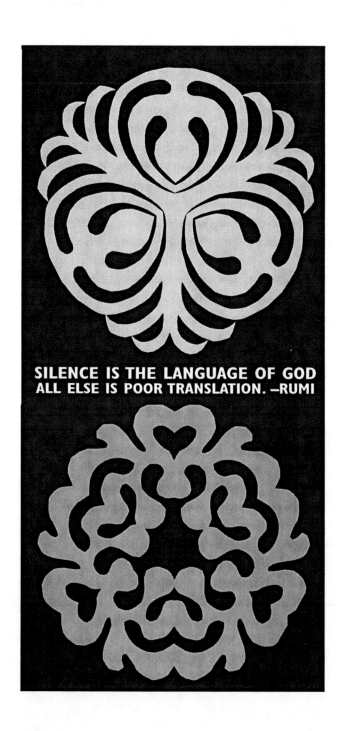

SILENCE IS THE LANGUAGE OF GOD
ALL ELSE IS POOR TRANSLATION. —RUMI

Markley Morris

15

OBEDIENCE

Letting go of perfection and reputation, I write a poem
just for God and me. The rest of you aren't even
allowed to listen in. The first words come to me—
a question of course (is there any other way to have
a conversation with God?). I set the words down
carefully, pen precise on the page, wanting
God to know I'm listening with all my heart, all my grief,
all my confusion. God says: Put them down. So I do.
I set my grief and confusion carefully beside me.
God says: Go back to the beginning. First words. Don't pick
them up; let your eyes sink into them, let your fingers
explore, learn the way of these first words and then follow
where they lead. Find the invisible path that winds
through all the disturbances, that forest of spines and thorns.
Follow the path across the plains of distractions and through
the city of judgment, past the palace of fear, and do not
enter the temple. Continue on out of the city into
the wilderness, an orchard of possibility. When
the path ends in some unknown place, take your
ignorance and skepticism out of the bag and gently
ever so gently set them down on that stump. Then
stand back, if you please, for this is the cathedral of
the Holy, and these gifts you have brought me are
precious in my sight. You are confused? So typical
of a human, always complicating things. Never mind.
Go sit under that tree and have some lemonade while I
have myself a Time here. And I say: Oh God, take thou
my unbelief and make me whole. And God says:
Oh Child. Drink your lemonade. Slip slowly into the simplicity
of sour and sweet, wet and dry. Drink it up. It's
your thirst, not I, that makes you whole.

Gyllian Davies

TWO HUNDRED BUDDHAS

Jerry Ellison-Green's story

Crossed backstraps of red galluses
Slipped into the catches on his clean denim overalls
Over a lighter blue cotton shirt.
"So: I'm an uneducated redneck Texan
And I enlisted right out of high school,
Trained and took off for Nam,

"I was a God-fearing Bible thumper
As well as a serious patriotic American
Teen-age hero hell-bent on war.
But fighting felt wrong to me. Couldn't deal with it.
Got to watching the Buddhists. Those monks—
They looked so brown and peaceful

"In their long robes. Kinda happy.
And me in my uniform. I wanted—something.
Didn't know what. Whatever it was they had.
So I asked this monk, how come, and how long would it take
To learn how to be a Buddhist. That guy—
He laughed. Told me 'One night.'

"I didn't believe him. He smiled,
Said, 'Come with me.' He took me to this storeroom—
A temple maybe? with two hundred Buddhas
All exactly alike. Sure surprised me.
He gave me some candles, said he'd come back, and left
While I spent the night inside

"Locked up with two hundred Buddhas—
I couldn't figure it. But I lit one of the candles
And held it up to each of them, seeing
Their curved eyelids. How they held their fingers.
The way they smiled. And by morning I knew them,
All two hundred, each one different.

"So the monk came back. He laughed.
He knew I'd get it. And I started laughing.
So here I am—happy as a monk,
A Vietnam veteran redneck Texas farmer
Buddhist."

Phyllis Hoge

A 23RD PSALM FOR THE PACIFIC NORTHWEST

The Earth is my mother, I shall not want.
She makes me lie down beneath the singing fir trees.
She leads me beside the white, rushing water.
She restores my soul.
She leads me to high, windy places, for my heart's ease.

Yea, though I walk through the valley in shadow and doubt,
I shall fear no ending.
For I am within You.
Your rocks and Your trees, they comfort me.
You have made space for me in Your secret places.
You cleanse my mind with green water.
My cup runneth over.
May wisdom and beauty lie before me on all the Ways of my life,
May I dwell at the heart of the World forever.

Amen.

Carol Virginia Ferm Herrick

A FRIEND OF GOD

Seeking is a lovely place to be. Seeking feels purposeful. Seeking feels safe. It asks me to keep looking, but puts little demand on me, especially when I don't really know what I am after. Even so, there are those quirks of dissatisfaction and those hints of absence which don't make much sense. The first hint fuels the continued hunt. The second bemuses.

Then it all crashes apart. Nothing holds and everything is wonderful. The presumption that my worth is nil evaporates. The close-held secret that I can't be loved is held up in the air and folded in invisible loving arms which tell another truth.

So *this* is what it means to be a friend of God. A lifetime's worth of assumptions about the world are dumped in an instant, overwhelmed by the power of unconditional love. I experience a gut comprehension that this is what I am called to be.

I guess you could say there are strings attached—the tethers of a hot air balloon rather than the bindings of a captive. I am told to stop being such a prickly jerk and sulking in a corner. Mend the relationships you've strained. Find words to speak of this!—to say what it is you've found as well as the need to remake your life.

Speak what it means to be a friend of God! That's the primary doing which arises from this core. Carry in your being and beneath all your words the pain of wandering lost and frightened. Share out of the isolation that was and the brokeness of being each in our worldly pursuits, hiding what we know in our hearts.

Walk in the shoes of those you used to mock and deride, accompanied by the other. Find out what it is to be friends with those you could not see as friends of God.

Stand in the knowledge that abundance is present in every heart, each linked to the next. Affirm the truth of the paradox that is at the core of each dichotomy that blinds us to the Seed. Know that there is a fullness that is more than minds can conceive. Know that we are asked to be present at the conception of a fresh way, where strength is to be found in our weaknesses, and in the mire of the swamp, our feet may be set on a rock.

Margery Post Abbott

MY ONLY HOPE

Standing next to the ocean has always reminded me of the enormity of God and my own insignificance. Lately, I have felt like God is the ocean and I am in it, being thrown against the rocks.

My fights with God usually go something like this:

God, I am not going to do that.

God, please don't make me do that.

God, do I really have to do that?

Okay, God, I will do it, but I am not going to be happy about it.

I get really angry with God sometimes, but that's okay. God can take it. And then when I am done, we continue on. At times, I hear a quieter voice from God, saying, "You know, we don't always have to do this the hard way..."

As a kid reading the Bible, I had a hard time with the command to love God. It made God seem needy and vain and I didn't want to love anyone who would demand love. This time through, I've started to see this differently. Loving makes us better people, the people God wants us to be.

I also didn't like the idea of God as a father. That description made me think of some distant, invisible disciplinarian. But what occurred to me recently is that God is family. Drive you crazy, call at the wrong time, you're-stuck-with-me kind of family. No one knows you quite like family, and in a pinch, there's no one I would rather have at my side.

Ashley Wilcox

WHAT I MEAN WHEN I TALK ABOUT GOD

these are excerpts from a journal of "definitions of god" that i kept for awhile. i know that god is vast and that i can only understand a little bit at a time, so i decided to record those little bits.

we all belong to god, and god belongs to all and if god is that mysterious and vast, it must be everything we can and can't imagine—everything we work together to discover—and to forget.

god is the wonderful—and the wonderful effects of forgiving the imperfect.

god is everything i'm too stubborn to let myself know.

god is having your heart busted open—and staying open. cracking open and letting go of who you are in order to take in something more vast.

god is complete vulnerability and complete strength. that is how god is love—and not control. you can't control what has busted you open. you can only stay open to it.

god is radical honesty. god is peering so far into yourself that you know there is nothing left to be afraid of. god is that in you that deeply resonates with other people. god is the hard and worthwhile work of creating real peace in ourselves, our personal relationships, our communities and our world. we have to be brave enough to face ourselves to learn that there is no other who can harm us.

i've been having a lot of internal arguments with atheists lately. because i think god is tremendously misunderstood—and I think what atheists reject is very frequently not god. it's the very rejectable way that god has been stolen and mishandled by many who claim religion.

prayer is not for god. it's for me. even if i go at prayer with the purest of intentions it's not actually doing anything for god. it's transforming me. the more i am grateful, the more i find to be grateful for. the more i ask for help, the more i find internally for strength and rest. god doesn't need appeasing.

god is everyone who has been through this before, and is going through it now. every reaction and action and the infinite similarities and differences. you can argue with god and rage at god, and god is everyone who has gotten just as pissed off as you.

there's the question of why call it god. isn't god dead, meaningless, a worthless concept? maybe, but I want to be in the history. i want to find my oneness with every human being who has been enlivened by the mystery. then maybe i'll be ready to explore my oneness with those who've given up.

i am enraged that god is used in the mouths of those who make these terrible systems exist. god is not that. god is not the inequities.

god is who we *have* to listen to or we are lost. even if the god-word drives you crazy, we all have in us something that will give us the answers if we just actually listen. and sometimes, they're scary, but they're the only things that will save us right now. some of us call that god, some of us call it ourselves, some of us call it both. but we need to listen.

we create god in our own images. that's all we can do with something so infinite. so, to make god more loving and forgiving, i have to be more loving and forgiving. we make the universe in our perceptions and our actions. the only way to make your ideal world is to live in it. the only way to live in it is to listen when god tells us to open up and love.

a god that doesn't make my world feel more like rejoicing doesn't feel like god to me.

i don't think belief in god is some alchemical mental trick. i don't

23

think you have to call anything "god," but i like talking about god. the word has a history i can stare at and discuss with other people. but i think belief in those three letters as a magic coin of recognition is dangerous.

many times when i think "god," i say "universe"—because the universe is vast and unknowable—and it's a fact. but the universe can be impersonal and my understanding of god isn't. my understanding of god is in the pulse of our interconnectedness. it's the holy, moving part of the space between you and me.

✻

today there was a latino man yelling on the bus, yelling to us "o childrens of israel," telling us to "shun the buddha and shun the kuram." telling us that marriage is between a man and a woman. telling us that if a tsunami comes "like in indonesia," it would be our fault. god would be punishing us.

i wanted to have the words and the bravery to address his fear. i wanted to have the integrity to stop mocking his mispronunciations in my head.

he told us that he loved us. when he got off the bus there was applause. some because it was quiet. some because they agreed with him. an african american woman said that there was nothing wrong with what he said.

i can't say i know god better than them. i am in a position of comparable power. how can that give me better access to god? but god seems bigger to me than that rage-filled fire. that rage-filled fire seems like so much not-god to me.

he said that god would transform us. every day i feel transformed by god.

my job is not to judge him. my job is to live my transformation, love fully, and not get sealed off in any of my fears. that's the transformation—the life beyond fear.

✻

i don't think religion in general or christianity in specific makes a person moral. but i think it keeps you both grounded and airy to feel that you are linked to god.

or at least that's how i perceive my experience right now. maybe i'm actually getting more smug. and maybe i could have felt buoyed in this way in a secular life. but i don't think i am smug right now, and i don't think i was buoyed in this way before. things still challenge me, but i feel ready for them in a different way. not terrified of the challenge— or of myself. i'm not in charge of things enough to destroy them.

it is healing to spend time putting the people i care about into the care of the universe. contemplating them and a universe of benevolence together is good for me.

thank you for taking care of my friends. thank you for making them who they are. help us continue to be full, real, and blessed.

i belong to a faith that believes in continuing revelation.

sometimes I feel so connected to god and what it's telling me through the universe. and sometimes the mystery is there—and theoretically i respect, love and honor the mystery—but it's a little exasperating to flounder.

where are you? what do you want? what am I supposed to do?

you can yell at, argue with, attempt to guilt-trip god. god can take it. you might even get closer. because god is your honesty about the world and if aspects seem false, they must stretch.

i don't want to stubbornly cling to my ideas of god. i want them to grow and shift. i don't want to ever make god less than me.

god is real. and by that i don't mean as opposed to imagined—I mean god is everything that is deep down truth. god is the part of eyes that is true—and the part of sand that is true—and the part of anger, ache, music, oranges, and caramelized onions that is true. maybe those are all the same truth or maybe they are all parts of one bigger one.

praying is asking what is the loving connection to that everything and how can I best help? what is the scariest, most me-less thing i can do? and having faith that you will still be you, enriched, afterwards.

faith is so funny. because it is challenging. it's believing that things could be better than they are—despite what it looks like—and also that where we are right now makes sense. that is challenging. because it looks pretty desperate a lot of the time.

but when you believe, you have been changed and are changing the world.

god is the space that opens up when there is truth.

god is more than easy listening—because god is more than easy. and yet, god is easier than anything else. how can i express that?

cubbie storm

QUAKERS

QUERIES

Do you clear a way for the Spirit, for the Living Silence, to enter your time of worship? How?

In what ways do you experience leadings or Divine guidance?

How does your Meeting nurture you and how do you nurture your meeting?

VESSELS

Before I came to California, I was an aquatic biologist, and I frequently wrote poetry while in the field. I now have access to clay and kilns so I also work in clay. Vessels are a form I have done for a long time, and considering humans as vessels for "that of light" or divine nature appeals to me.

Pat Howe

WHAT COMES IN SILENCE

What comes in silence as we wait?
Whose whisper? Grip? Whose quickened breath?
Whose tidal surge pulls on our blood?
That shakes our rustling leaves and speaks:

I Am, the wind, the rush of rain
I Am, the burning spear of light
I breathe your life and plow your death.
And harvest flowers on your grave.

Listen to My urgent blooming
Listen to My roots run through you
I pulse in blood, proclaim in bone
Sing throbbing ivies through your veins

Listen... Listen...
Hush.
Now, speak.

Rob Pierson

THE PEACEABLE KINGDOM

When Edward Hicks the Quaker died
Friends mourned the preacher more than the artist,
and he himself had scorned his paintings,
the dozens of variants of his dreamy creation
compiled of images from old etchings,
his talent nothing but a "munkey's art..."
sufficient "to imitate but never life impart."
He'd have put brakes on his imagination if he could.

But he gave the pictures to friends to inspire them
to master their passions, find "peace of soul"
the way the lion and lamb had, and the way
William Penn and the Indians had, as can be seen
down in the lower left corner under the elms,
such peace as needs no oath taken. The children –
four in some versions, only a pair or just one in others –
look so angelic and joyous in white frocks as they romp
among beasts and in trees and in air that they seem
already ripe to skip earthly life and proceed straight
to heaven, leaving elders to deal with the problems.

In a true Christian kingdom, Hicks averred,
there would be no such a thing as a fine painter,
for that is "one of those trifling, insignificant arts...
never of any substantial advantage to mankind,"
and even worse, "the inseparable companion
of voluptuousness and pride," having "presaged
the downfall of empires and kingdoms..."

Even worse, the painter could not resist writing poems,
but his peaceable kingdom was rather poorly policed,
permitting this artist to practice even more than he preached.

David Ray

WHY I WANT TO BE A QUAKER

My partner has joined
I've been coming for years
I enjoy the community
So what are my fears?

It's way too religious, they use the word God
There are too many pamphlets
Should I wear my hair bobbed?

I might not be active enough,
My politics not clear.
But I'm in favor of peace
No matter what year.

The way things are decided
Is decidedly slow.
Is it worth it to listen and struggle
To include all who know?

The building is crumbling
The people keep coming
It's bound to be work
Even bringing the snacks
Has gotten too lax
But I'm not going to shirk.

No, I've decided to cast my lot
With the folks who don't talk (much)

I'm asking to be accepted
Flawed as I might be
Olympia Monthly Meeting
Can I join thee?

Beta Anderson

FOX BONES

Christ is the Light of the World and lighteth everyone that cometh
  into the world.
This Light is within you.
This Light will show you all Righteousness and unrighteousness.
It will show you how you have spent your time,
And how you have acted,
All you have hurt, all your mean and selfish thoughts, all your vain
  words,
Which is your condition, living apart from Delight.
In that Light wait,
That you may receive Power and Strength
To stand against what the Light makes manifest.
Here is the first step to true Peace... wait in the Light.

This Light is present with you in all the workplaces
And in all the actions of your daily life,
And in your conscience.
It will check you and reprove you for speaking or acting selfishly
Or with a mean spirit.
Here is your Teacher... within.
Therefore wait within to know the mysteries opened within you.
For Faith by personal experience is the gift of God to you,
And comes by hearing the Word preached in your heart... within.

The Light is within which shines in your darkness,
  but your darkness cannot comprehend it.
Christ, the Way, the Truth, and the Life is within, and his working is
  within,
And the sure Word of prophecy is within,
And the Day to dawn and the Day Star to arise is within,
And the Law and the Covenant is within,
And the Seed of God is within, and all the promise to the Seed of God
  is within.
The light of God's Glory is within,
The heavenly Treasure is within,
The Unction is within,

The Bread of Life is within,
And the spiritual communion is within, not in the flesh but in the
 Spirit.

The Cross is within that crucifies the fearful self... the enemy of the
 soul.
The Sword of the Spirit and spiritual Armor that shields and
 defends your soul
Is not in a Book outside of you, but within in the Spirit.
The Book declareth of them,
But the Sword and Amour are within in the Power of God.
Wait in the Light that discovers the error and the lie in you,
And in the Light that raises up a daily Cross to crucify the selfish will,
That would rule you with fear, and lust and resentment.
This Light will set a Watch over you, over your thoughts and actions.
A Power will arise within to deliver you from temptations,
A Power to work out the selfish part from the center of your being.

Therefore, all you that love the Light within you, stand still in it,
Out of all your own thoughts, your self justifications, the devotion
 given to self,
Out of what self would have you imagine you need.
Wait.
Wait for the true Power and Strength, Joy and Comfort to your souls,
Which no man can give, but God alone does give it freely
To all that wait in the Light... and obey.

All you who love the Light and obey it will be led out of darkness,
Will be led away from the corrupt deeds of self into the Light of Life,
Into the Way of Peace,
And into the Life and Power of Truth.
This Light, If you love and obey it, will lead you from your will-
 worship,
And the lifeless, deceitful customs of the world that surrounds you.It
will teach you to worship God in Spirit and in Truth,
And you will know what it is to be ordained in the open and
 authentic Life
And in the Spirit's Mystery.

This is a personal and poetic transcription of the teaching of George Fox from letter Number 23, 51 A in The Annual Catalogue of Fox's Papers of The Swarthmore Manuscripts *and is taken from T. Canby Jones' collection of the pastoral letters of George Fox,* Power of the Lord Is Over All *(1989, Friends United Press), p. 474. I have tried to keep to Fox's language but have freely inserted new wording that speaks to my condition where I thought newer or more personal words were needed.*

Reading Fox may cause us to forget that he was a powerful speaker. There is a natural cadence in Fox's writing that must have come from his constant speaking. It is my hope that my transcription will make that cadence plain; bringing out the power of Fox's voice to speak today to our condition. Fox is always better read aloud.

Robert Griswold

Recent years have seen the rise of radio spots, websites and a book series devoted to "This I Believe" – the collection of individual statements of core values and beliefs that Edward R. Murrow pioneered back in 1951. Many of the statements are profoundly felt and deeply moving. But, as a Quaker, I sometimes wonder whether our own series might have a more apophatic title, something like: "Why Believe?"

Why believe? Seriously... stop a moment. Why believe? From our earliest days, Quakers questioned beliefs, questioned "notions" that distracted from direct experience.

I grew up in a world of beliefs, a religious home, dominated by dinner-time Bible readings, bedtime prayer, Sunday sermons and Sunday school. It was the 1970s, and in our catechisms and statements of faith, we swore to the right beliefs—the beliefs that would make right a world gone wrong, a world shredded by a million other heartfelt beliefs. White prejudice clashed with black pride while anti-war protestors shouted in the face of nationalistic fervor. Families dreaded feminism; capitalists dreaded communism. Catholics battled Protestants, and Protestant battled amongst themselves. It was us versus them and, ultimately, us versus us. Everyone killed and was killed, and everywhere in the name of Peace, Truth, Justice, or, sometimes, the American Way. What we said we believed felt utterly at odds with what we did.

And then, one summer evening, as crickets chirred at the edge of the woods, I was feeding the fish in our neighbor's goldfish pond as the sun sank slowly behind the trees. At one moment, I was standing by the shaded pool, watching orange and white shadows of fish as the light shone around me. In the next, something was shining right through me, melting away my beliefs, melting away me, until all that remained was the Light, nothing but Light.

Years later, I found many others who spoke from experience of the spiritual, the mystical and the apophatic: St. John of the Cross, Julian of Norwich, Jelaluddin Rumi, John Muir. Thomas Merton climbed his Seven Storey Mountain only to take photographs of a swept porch, fields in winter, and chopped wood. He once took a picture of a metal hook hanging down from a clear sky and labeled it "the only known photograph of God."

Do I believe in God? There's no need; I've seen the photograph! And I've laughed in recognition of what lies beyond. What is, Is. Belief costs extra. The philosopher Krishnamurti wandered the world declaring truth a pathless land. Lao Tsu, writing thousands of years earlier said much the same: watch out for those who say they know the way.

Navajos walk in Beauty, and Quakers keep to the Light, but believing much about the Beauty or the Light adds nothing to them.

Navajos walk in Beauty, and Quakers keep to the Light, but believing much about the Beauty or the Light adds nothing to them. What is, Is, just as It has insisted since Moses came upon the burning bush. And It will continue to be what It is, despite our belief. In Meeting, we simply wait.

Now in my forties, with my own children struggling to grow whole, I see this world even more polarized, blinded, and blown to pieces by belief. I was a few miles outside Washington D.C. when some believing themselves agents of grace plowed an airplane into those believing themselves safe and secure. Beliefs have never made us right, nor kept us safe.

Rumi wrote:

Out beyond ideas of wrong-doing
and right-doing, there is a field.

I'll meet you there.

As I walk under the beautiful open skies of New Mexico, watching aspen leaves emerge in the spring, listening to them clink quietly in the summer breeze, and seeing them turn golden in autumn, falling to the forest floor, I know we can meet in that field beyond ideas. In fact, in Meeting we seek to sit in that field together and feel the breeze, the ruach, breath of God. The Beauty and the Light are already there; we just have to drop the beliefs that separate and blind us.

Rob Pierson

37

The first time I came to a Friends Meeting is still exemplary to me. I had come to get a friend of mine to stop nagging me to, "go to Quaker Meeting. You'll find a lot to agree with." I had turned my back on organized religion and anything with Christian roots after leaving the Episcopal Church's homophobia. I had found no one whose teachings matched what I had found in Jesus's own words. None seemed interested in the activism and pacifism that I found central.

As we walked in through the courtyard, I asked the friend, "So what do we do now? Stand when we sing and kneel when we pray?" And he replied, "We sit and meditate for an hour. In silence."

If he had not had the car keys, I probably would have raced out the door. But we were halfway into the Worship Room and they were closing the doors behind me—I was trapped!

Somehow I managed to sit still for more than 15 minutes, the longest I had ever been able to "meditate" before. At some point I realized I was comfortable and the silence was buoying me up while I floated in inchoate thoughts. I found myself reflecting on three challenges I faced in my life at that time.

After about thirty more minutes, someone stood and spoke, without tremolo or tears, about the first question on my mind, pondering very similar concerns. I was surprised, but found her words useful and continued to mull them over until I found myself reflecting again on the second worry. At that moment an elderly man stood in the far corner and said about three sentences, in a sort of prayer, that went bull's-eye into my preoccupation. "Well! Two out of three... Not bad!" I thought to myself.

Then the children came in as they used to for closing. There was great shuffling and shushing, and I distracted myself thinking of the afternoon to come. Just as the hour was almost up, another Friend stood and, making some comparison with children and their restless growing, skewered my final problem. Soon thereafter handshakes began but I was still stunned and needed to sit with my thoughts for a while more.

On my way to the Social Hall later, I looked over the rack of fliers and realized that I was indeed home among my own kind. Every meeting since has been different and the same. What a blessing it has been.

What happens to me in Quaker worship? Like others I have a preferred routine on Firstday morning: funnies OK; news no—too jangling. Radio classical music fine; ads bad. Quiet breakfast and vitamins, yes; extra cuppa coffee with sugary roll, no way. I sit in about the same area week after week, the familiarity comforting me and providing just the stimuli I need, although the point has moved like magnetic north slowly around the room over the years. I shut my eyes to cut to the alpha waves and to take in the crows' scratches on the skylight and the roar of traffic in canal and freeway. I cup one hand in another or open them to receive the universe's gifts while steadying my breathing to a count of One, One, One, One, One, we are One. My mantra almost every day for fifteen years' worship is the prayer of Francis of Assisi: "Make me an instrument of Thy peace."

Opening my eyes I mentally greet familiar faces and hold their lives and needs in the Light. I pray for a long list of absent friends. I worry about the work on my desk at home and the next deadline. Sometimes, like others, I am distracted by sex, drugs and rock'n'roll. Other times I feel dry and disconnected or wish I were outside in the sunshine. But usually I reach a point of expectation: something good is about to happen and I am ready.

Sometimes what comes is gathered, covered silence, as depicted in the lithograph of "The Presence in the Midst." Others it is a message that reveals my own mind. A favorite metaphor of mine is from a Friend who shared that her washing machine had overflowed because she had tried to stuff two loads' worth of dirty laundry in at once— our lives and our minds are much the same way and she prayed that we could be tubs with enough room for the Living Water to fill our worship.

But what happens to me? Where does that constantly distracting ego go so that *me* is no longer the most important thing in life for an hour at least once a week? Why do others seem to speak to my varying condition with such accuracy? Why is it that God's grace and hope for life ahead become apparent when we are together like this?

How is it that without my wanting it a message can come through me so clearly and so fast that I have to ask others what "I" said? And I am no longer what fills me? Ask God—only She knows.

Sometimes I experience slowly opening from outside in to the Truth and seeing. It may arise from another's vocal ministry which echoes leadings that have also come to me. Other times it arises seemingly out of my own mind's silence once I have fully centered. Then something that is True begins to form into words. Often others' words come from my memory in songs, poems, quoted epigrams or lines from scripture (the Bible or other inspired writings) to incarnate the idea and help propel it forward in my consciousness. It may be a new insight or a realization of a connection that had not been apparent to me before.

Once I have a grasp on what the message is, I usually test it. Is it for me or for us all? If it's mine I spend time contemplating it. If it feels like it wishes to be shared, I challenge it to prove that it's more useful than the rich silence—because it's very rare for a message to come unless the Meeting is gathered and we are holding each other with tenderness. Paradox usually means closeness to truth. "Joy is the ineffable sign of the Presence of God."

When it is time to share, I usually find myself rising out of my chair while still trying to figure out what it is that I have to share. Sometimes I don't get it out, or my words get mixed up or the main point comes after so many steps that I forget to make it. In any case, I try to be just a useful channel for the Truth, after which I feel emptied once again. And that's good, and I celebrate life.

D. Pablo Stanfield

After North Pacific Yearly Meeting Annual Session a few years ago, I was talking with a Friend who is new to Quakers. She expressed concern and dismay after attending an interest group on the Christian-Universalist split. The difference among Friends was difficult for her.

I felt an imperative to resolve this issue for myself years ago when it first came to my attention. John Woolman spoke to my condition when he wrote, "There is a principle which is pure, placed in the human mind, which in different places and ages hath had different names. It is deep and inward, confined to no forms of religion, nor excluded from any where the heart stands in perfect sincerity. In whomsoever this takes root and grows, of what nation soever, they become brethren." I set out to explore what this has meant and means now for me personally.

I am a Christian because that is how I was raised. It is the culture I came from, the belief system whose language I am familiar with, and through which I "approach" a dialogue with the Divine.

I am also a Universalist because I believe that God reveals truth to all people, whether Hindu, Muslim, Jew, Buddhist, or Native American. Therefore, all belief systems are avenues through which we can all discover more about and grow in the knowledge of our common creator.

In my worship group at Annual Session, someone spoke of our obligation to speak when something just doesn't sit right. To me this may be a clue that one is being moved by the Spirit to engage in dialogue.

I wanted to say that we are equally obligated to listen. Through this speaking and listening we engage in a dialogue that enables us to discern that of God in ourselves, in each other, and in our corporate body. This is holy work. I believe this obligation carries over into the larger world of God's creation, to engage in the process of dialogue and discernment with people of other cultures and belief systems, to grow in the knowledge and love of God, and to learn what God would have us do, individually and corporately.

Belief systems are from humankind and are therefore limited. Faith is from God and is unlimited. My faith will not be limited by my belief.

I recently watched the Dalai Lama in a video titled *Compassion in Exile*. He appeared to me to be clearly a man of God. I saw and heard him and other Tibetans speak of forgiveness of the Chinese who are destroying the Tibetan temples and their culture and forcing the Tibetans into exile. I saw more than forgiveness. There was genuine concern about what will happen to the Chinese because of their actions, as the Tibetans have a strong belief that what one does to others will eventually be visited on oneself.

Is this forgiveness, love, and compassion not from God? I know of no human belief system in which forgiveness and concern greater than this are expressed. Is this forgiveness, love, and compassion not valid or not from God because it is not from a Christian belief system?

Can we who are Christian or Hindu or Jew or Muslim not add to our concepts of forgiveness, love, and compassion through knowledge and belief from another culture and religion?

This is only one of many examples that I find from other belief systems that do not take away from or diminish my belief, but only add to and enhance my faith. I am discerning more and more that my/our God is truly a universal God who reveals truth to all people. We can only enhance our knowledge of this Divine Presence by engaging in this discovery of what is being revealed through all of God's people.

I also believe that, as children of one God, whatever separates us from each other also separates us from God.

We speak of Birthright Friends, as those who are born into the Religious Society of Friends, into that belief system. I like to keep in mind that we are all Birthright Children of God, born into an inherent knowledge of and faith in a Divine Presence that is present in, transcends, and encompasses all of our human systems of belief. If we truly knew and understood this, what might it allow us to accomplish in this world? I believe that we could truly become the People of God that God desires us to be.

Jami Hart

IN THE WORLD

QUERIES

Do you leave room for deep listening in the midst of a busy life?

How does your faith encourage you to respond to the beauty and the mystery, as well as the pain and suffering, that surrounds you?

Do you acknowledge and witness to that of God in others?
Can you acknowledge and witness to that of God in yourself?

PILGRIM OFFERINGS AT CHIMAYO, NEW MEXICO

Rob Pierson

THE SURRENDER GARDEN

for Wendell Berry

I farm a room-sized plot of earth
where once a factory stood.
In spring, I'm met by eager volunteers—
onions and leeks, swiss chard and kale
green and sweet as those in paradise.

But as I turn the soil for the first time,
bricks the size and shape of potatoes
stick in my digger's stubborn teeth.
My brow sweats. My winter-weary muscles ache.
I feel the effects of the fall.

My seeds are scattered to the sound
of kids and cars, trolleys and boom boxes.
I use my hands instead of a digger
because I love to mold and stroke the earth,
to feel it touch my skin.
I sit in my garden like a kid in a sandbox
and think of my Greek grandfather
for whom gardening was no game.

With the sun and rains
weeds rise up like angry peasants
insisting on their squatter's rights.
I can't blame them.
I've been an absentee.
Down on my knees, I make a space
for my seedlings as I pull the weeds
carefully by the roots,
roots that go on and on
like my compulsions and obsessions.
This is the work that never seems to end,
the work my father and his father handed down.

Some evenings I come here simply to sit alone,
and watch things grow.

It's quiet and still as a church.
At the far end of the garden
a woman waters her flowers,
and the smell of wet earth rises
like a prayer, an offering,
into the darkening sky.

Anthony Manousos

OUT OF THE SILENCE

On First Day a man stood up and said
"Our task, Friends, is to be worthy
of what we were spared for!" That's all

the man said, and failed to explain what
he had in mind or provide any context.
I have heard lines like that in the street

or in bars, and assumed they were uttered
by those who were half insane, perhaps
some bearded fool muttering to himself.

But then again, there might be a context
one does not speak of, for it's odd how
life and light waver, how one is spared

or is not – the diagnosis outlived or war
survived or the dread nuclear nightmare
delayed long beyond probabilities although

there is nothing on earth not hostage still.
The man rose to his feet on First Day —
a morning that had somehow arrived

as promised, grace enough. But another
war was in progress and each day's evil
more than sufficient to balance its blessings.

David Ray

TAPESTRY OF SILENCE & WORK

Small pockets of silence punctuate my day:
Its weft bringing strength.

Muno's amazed whisper "Beautiful" her only English
At hearing her first concert a world away from Somalia
The blinzes Maria brought -
Her recipe all the way from Siberia.
Syncopated Chinese as Chau Anh says,
"That not important" to my frets,
Whose people invented thousand-year eggs.

The immigrant father in red, white and blue
Starched spotless United States of America t-shirt
Saying in his soft tongue,
"I never go to school. My son go to school now."

I am left full to breaking
I can't swallow another thing
And I can't decide if I'm full from joy or grief.

Annette Carter

INSTRUCTIONS FOR A DARK NIGHT

Some black night
Stretch out on a summer field,
Breathe grassiness into every bone.
Then the deep ocean of darkness will bloom
Stars beyond count,
Ancient beyond imagination.

Wait for stillness,
Watch the scatter of stars slowly crawl from
Horizon to horizon,
Feel earth spin through deep
Darkness in a cadence of
Time longer
Than human memory.

We are only children on the shore
Imagining the vastness before us
Just beyond our fingertips.

Annette Carter

THAT WHICH BOGGLES

I received the email from my friend the science teacher on Darwin's birthday. He was expressing admiration for Quakers. He had read a bit by some British Friend stating that Quakers had no quarrel with Mr. Darwin or the Theory of Evolution. He was impressed and was telling me so. I accepted his kudos and for the sake of integrity stated that there were some Friends who might not have much truck with Darwin, but that I was not one of them.

My friend is no kind of religionist. He is intelligent, gentle and kind. He is tolerant of those like me who live their lives in conversation with what I am sure he thinks of as an elaborate imaginary friend called God. But he feels no need of such supernatural supports.

Yet I am not sure that he and I have no common spiritual ground. Because I have heard him describe what I would call a mystical experience, what early Friends would call an opening. He is a science teacher, secondary school. He came to it late after another career. He came to it because he had continuing and powerful experiences in the pursuit of science. I have heard him describe the experience of discovery of that which boggles the mind. He describes this experience with deep passion and obvious joy. He can describe being a good enough student, an attentive enough observer, that he reaches a plane where he bumps into truth so amazing that all the mind can do is boggle—gaze in rapt awe—try to accept what it can only incompletely comprehend. He describes the desire of all scientists to take that comprehension just one step farther than the boggle point. He calls this science. I, of course, have the same experience and call it religion. But I recognize that his science is one very fine religion.

The Worship of That Which Boggles has meetinghouses—classrooms and laboratories. It has rituals and methodologies. If you advance far enough you get vestments—lab coats and regalia. It has acolytes. My friend is there for the acolytes. He is the master of novices. He teaches all his students, but he watches for the nascent believers, the ones who get excited when they near the boggle point. And he is an evangelist. He actively attempts to introduce them to TWB. He knows that not all will be boggled—that only a few will pursue further bogglement, that fewer still will make it their life's passion. But he scatters his seed widely and harvests whereever life sprouts.

His religion, like mine, believes in the doctrine of continuing revelation. That what we discern, and test, and live into will develop and change and grow as our understanding grows. We both believe in Truth, and we both believe it is blasphemy to claim that you have grasp of the entire truth.

I have worshipped at this altar. For me it was college and the double slit light experiment where light behaves like a brazen floozy, and shows you wave or particle depending on what you ask for. She cannot be both and yet she is. I have been boggled. I occasionally worship with the bogglers still. Whenever someone will teach me at the Zen beginner's level that I need. That is why I like to have my friend over for an ecumenical dinner. He is a fine preacher, and I happily sit under his preaching.

I believe that his Boggler and mine are one. I do work in a different department. The division of hearts and souls, tech support, specifically. I am but a lab assistant in the laboratory of sanctification. I help people when their work gets stuck. I know some best practices that produce reliable results. I help them check their numbers. I listen to their reports and give feedback. But once in a while I still get into that Holy of Holies of pure bogglement.

I have stood with souls who are despairing, screamingly suicidal, no hope, no comfort, no reason to live. They stand facing a precipice, contemplating an all or nothing experiment in permanent pain management. I stand shoulder to shoulder with them, but facing the other way– pointing towards life. What always amazes me is how these souls can be simultaneously and completely committed to opposing, contradictory aims. They want to die and they want to live. It cannot be both ways, but it is. I see wave, they see particle. And then if I am very blessed, in that moment of paradox, they take my hand and take one step away from the edge. Where the strength comes from to do this I do not know. But I know that I am boggled every time. And I know that my simple attention, my observation of their pain, changes something. That is pastor Schroedinger's sermon, I believe.

Peggy Senger Parsons

SWIMMING POOL GODDESS

Sometimes I swim to help with the pain. When I feel good enough to get my body down to the public pool, slipping into cool water can almost make me feel well again, for a spell. Coolness quiets down the heat in my lower intestines and lets me concentrate on here and now. Moving through the water, I am swallowed up. The lovely sensations buffer me. When I feel the water flowing over my skin, I'm not lost in the pain and it's not awful to be where I am.

Feeling better lasts for the entire time I am swimming and, if I'm lucky, a little while afterwards, too—maybe thirty minutes more. Every moment that I am not bombarded by rawness, burning, or itching entrains another site in my brain to live somewhere besides the hurt. That is good. A secondary benefit to swimming is that sometimes, I meet very interesting people at the pool.

Like this one day. Turning to breathe, my face lifts up from the water and I am gazing at her towering above me. She is too much for me to take in all at once. My eyes must take the climb slowly to let in all of her impressive figure. They rise up past feet planted sturdily upon the water's edge, following the contours of her powerfully constructed legs, ascending to the fecundity of a torso rounded with youth and sensuality. Full figure molded into a red dot polka dot bikini suit. Not the itsy bitsy, teeny weeny, yellow polka dot bikini of yore, but an equally fabulous temple of red polka dottedness. My vision dapples in Seurat-style to recreate a luscious Renoira/Rubenesque.

Her presence is overwhelming. Really, I can scarcely breathe in Her company! As I stared, the swimming pool goddess began to shine and grow brighter than other objects in my visual field. I wasn't sure, but was fuzzy light emanating from the outline of her skin? Trying to recall if it really is true that effervescence is a mark of youthful vitality. After all, young people are often referred to as bubbly, aren't they? Or perhaps the sparkling white light is simply a function of hopelessly nearsighted/farsighted eyes distorting an object without their familiar spectacles? Just *what* is shining? I swear the girl at the pool is sporting a whole body halo! I imagine the disciples seeing Jesus Christ bathed in a halo like this. Is this brightness, this radiance, what passes for an aura?

My spirit vascillates between appreciation and awe to separation. I chastise myself for what I am not. Behold beauty and then hold it out at arms length. Beauty, fulfillment and grace have receded to the outside world and are no longer available. At least, not through *you*.

Envy pierced my skinny old bones and coalesced into a long thin snakelike rod that beat me like a hickory stick. *Why* aren't I like that anymore? What happened to my youthful beauty and awesome power? I am left in a shell weathered with fifty-four seasons of stress and disappointment, and battered with five seasons of unrelenting pain.

Almost drowning in destructive thoughts, I must make the effort to shift concentration. So here I am, consciously turning my vision away from her to sensations of my body moving through water. I kick my feet hard to increase resistance on the inner thighs.

When I look up again, the girl is gone. Toweling off, I move to the spa tub for some heat therapy. Securing my glasses in one of the cubbies is easier than finding a safe spot for them on the edge of a swirling heat pool. Dimly, I look around and what do my clouded eyes land upon? Yes… of course. Her.

My pool Goddess is now diva of the hot tub with an entourage of one. She is talking intimately with some guy, some young guy, her boyfriend, I guess. I nod a casual greeting to the fuzzy images as I slide into the spa. The quiet bubbles are most peaceful and the heat is relaxing deep down to my bones. Ahhh.

Opening my eyes, I see the Goddess chatting lightly, easily, with the boyfriend. She is moving, slithering salaciously in circles all around the guy, like a charmed snake. Except she is the one doing the charming.

The boyfriend leaves and she walks boldly across the hot tub to stand in front of me. She's right there, in front of me, not three inches away. She is speaking, and near enough so that even my strongly nearsighted eyes can focus on her face.

Without warning, my attention converges into knifelike clarity. Standing so close now, uncomfortably so, I can count ten pimples caked with make-up. Layers of foundation mockingly frame and highlight more blemishes. Close up, her countenance is not handsome, not attractive, not fine-looking, not even healthy. Face to face, my Goddess is flushed, unevenly mottled, puffed up around the eyes. My velvety image of Beauty has sharpened onto a pockmarked moon balanced on top of a heavy, not heavenly, body. The face of the moon shines crusty and red, and bears a strained expression of *pleeezelikeme*. Pleading. Beseeching. Not quite demanding.

"Yes?" I say. I look at her and for the life of me, I cannot figure out why she would be telling me that somebody threw a cigarette into the pool.

"What!?" I sputtered, jolted by the unlikely unreality of reality.

"Somebody threw a cigarette into the pool, well not a cigarette, but you know, a match. Ewww! I fished it out."

"Thanks," I responded in a sort of daze.

Later on, showering in the locker room, I hear something. I almost think what I "hear" is only a song that I am singing silently to myself, but no. Someone in the locker room is singing and her chorus is bouncing off the walls. Over and over she chants,

> *Could there be some God, divine entity or other awareness who loves me more than I can or will ever know? It's hard to believe that if I am loved, I would continue to suffer so much physical pain.*

Jesus loves you more than you will know...
Jesus loves you more than you will know...
Jesus loves you more than you will know...

Does anyone, could someone love me more than I will know? Could there be some God, divine entity or other awareness who loves me more than I can or will ever know? It's hard to believe that if I am loved, I would continue to suffer so much physical pain. I really haven't been that bad of a human being, you know. Is my pain some kind of blessing in disguise, as some of those damned unsympathetic New Age pundits admonish?

Oh... My... God. My swimming pool Goddess is the one who is singing. The Glowing One, my so-ugly-she's-cute beauty. She's here. Surely she must symbolize some special kind of message just for me. The problem is that if she does represent some epiphany, I have no clue as to what the message is supposed to be. I don't get it at all.

And here she is, walking up to me, asking, "Do you know who sang Jesus loves you more than you will know?"

Simon and Garfunkel, I tell her. My voice is calm, masking a slight trace of scorn. How unbelievable to be so young that you don't recognize the song!

Without missing a beat, she asks me what lyrics come next... after the part about, "Jesus loves you more than you will know? Does it go... Oh hello?" She has been asking everyone, she tells me, "because I can't get the song out of my head."

To make up for my scorn, I suggest in my most pleasant social voice that she can probably check out the full lyrics on the internet.

Blissfully ignorant, she kindly throws me a sincere shout out of thanks as she drifts out of the locker room. No sooner does she leave than inner demons start up again. Is *this* my message?! What the hell am I supposed to learn from this?!

While I'm raging and ranting inside, the swimming pool angel calls back to me sweetly, You know, you are so cute, so easy to talk to. I feel I can just come up and ask you about anything.

Is that really true, am I easy to talk to? I wonder.

When I got home I couldn't stop thinking about the girl at the pool. I called my husband at work, and some friends who I rarely see to tell them about her. My animated accounts couldn't begin to touch on the imagery and mystery and presence and vitality that she symbolizes to me. Is my swimming pool Goddess powerful and commanding or is she pitiful and lost? Both seem to be true, yet neither set of adjectives can touch how she touched my humanness. If her apparition carries a message for me, it has to be something of a paradox.

What was her story? What is mine?

The next day, I felt compelled to return to the pool. A visceral, deep physical yearning pulled me to go swimming again. So I go to the pool, begin swimming and find she isn't there.

She's at the hot tub! Swimming pool Goddess is huddling familiarly, with a different guy this time. My first thought is, Wow! Does she get around!? That must be what it's like to be young. Which I am not. Familiar ways to beat myself up inside.

I sink down, deeper down, the water muffles disturbing echoes bouncing off the community area. Today, I watch her dance of engagement. As she sidles closer, the guy edges further and further away. They play the cat and mouse game way halfway round the rim of the tub until he escapes off the far edge. Unfazed, she easily turns to an elderly woman on her other side, like nothing awkward or unpleasant happened at all.

Someone is tapping my shoulder... the real live touch of the swimming pool girl. Pimply sweet, blotchy and red like yesterday, also curvy and youthful, young and timid. Telling me something. important.

"What is it about you?" she asks. "You just have a glow about you. Do you know you have a glow about you?"

Surprised, my first thought is to wonder if this is a come-on or trap. You can't just say to an old sick woman, "you just have a glow about you." But this time I consciously stop the mental gremlin and I decide to let this real life experience in. I accept her comment at face value.

Maybe I do have a glow. My friend, Pam, once told me I looked radiant in silent worship. She told me this at the same time that my subjective sitting experience was of someone screaming inside for relief, trying to find one moment when I didn't hurt. Maybe pain radiates an energy that looks like Light to others.

Then it dawned on me—she was the one with the aura. Her glow is how she first manifested. It is what attracted me so strongly in the first place. So I tell her so in as many words.

"*You* are the one who glows—that's exactly how you looked to me when I first saw you." I remember distinctly, her body was filled with light radiating from within.

"You were glowing," I tell her.

At first sighting she was shining like an angel. At the time, I thought it was sex, or beauty, or youthful vigor, but maybe her life just... glows.

"Really?!" she voices shy disbelief. "I don't feel that at all." Withdrawing into reticence and doubt. Her movements like a turtle curling into a shell. Her pain, though not physical like mine, is palpable. A very small part of her reaches out for rescue. So I just continue telling her my truth.

"You have the glow. I saw it," I testify to her. "Yes, you definitely have a glow, I can see it," my voice continues, and then I realize I'm on a roll here. "Maybe it's just that we just can't see our own glow. Maybe I'm seeing my own radiance in you, and the sparkle you see in me is really you. We are just reflections of each other, like mirrors. Maybe... it's easier to recognize in others what we are not ready to see in ourselves. One of my teachers, Tina, told me this profundity. And of course there is the often used Hindi greeting, 'Namaste,' which means something like, 'I behold in you what is in me,' and we are beautiful. We are one."

"So you mean everyone has a glow? Even me?" asks my swimming pool Goddess, ever so earnestly.

Yes, everyone, I nod with certainty, not knowing where my conviction comes from.

Smiling and glowing, she immediately spins out of my trajectory and turns herself all the way around by 180 degrees. She is straight on facing the only man left in the hot tub. "Do you know?...", she sidles up to the new guy and smiles. "Do you know, she says, ever so sweetly, "Do you know that you have a glow about you?"

Marian Wolfe Dixon

Stehekin, a remote mountain village fixed in an earlier time, taught me how to survive in the world today. Located in the North Cascades of central Washington, this community of less than 100 year-round residents is a place and a way of being. People who've been there awhile talk of being "Stehekinized."

Translated as "the way through," Stehekin once was a passageway at the end of 55-mile-long Lake Chelan for Skagit and Salish Indians. Later, highways were blasted through parts of the North Cascades, but none ever made it to Stehekin. Today, most people get "uplake" by a commercial passenger-only ferry that makes one trip daily. Others arrive by float plane, the hearty by hiking a full day over National Park and Forest Service trails.

Telephone lines from the "downlake" world never made it to Stehekin, and there aren't any cell towers, either. A single public telephone, for outgoing long distance calls only, haltingly relays voices via satellite when messages beyond Stehekin are urgent. Internet service has arrived recently, but just for those who install a satellite dish.

It was to this tiny, isolated village that my family and I moved in search of our own "way through" disillusionment. In May 1994, my husband and I quit our jobs in human services, found renters for our house, and prepared our twin son and daughter to enter seventh grade in the valley's one-room, kindergarten-through-eighth-grade school. Our transition was eased by a support committee from our Quaker Meeting, the encouragement of family and friends, and the availability of a rental house and jobs that first summer.

We had gotten to know the people and the way of life in Stehekin over ten years of vacationing in both summer and winter, so we didn't have many illusions about living so far removed from mainstream America. We learned during one July visit that we could cope with picking up our groceries at the boat three or four days after mailing our order and blank check to the Safeway store at the other end of the lake. We survived mosquitoes in droves and temperatures in the upper 90's without air conditioning. During winter holidays there we experienced extended power outages, the challenges of waking to three feet of fresh snow, and the trials of driving vintage vehicles over narrow, snow-packed village roads. We had heard springtime was wet, muddy, and filled with flooding dangers, and that fall, with its warm days, crisp nights, and spectacular colors, rarely lasted long enough to complete preparations for winter. I fretted about the lack of easy access to everything, especially emergency medical care, but I trusted the Stehekin spirit of interdependence would tolerate our inexperience and support us with the lessons we would learn there.

Mostly, though, I wanted a break. For twenty years I had worked as a nurse, primarily in public health. In my teens, I had felt called to a healing profession. Later, I realized I was led to serve the poor by being at their bedsides, visiting in their homes, and advocating for their care. I believed I had to witness to suffering to bring about health and wholeness. I felt deep affinity with the people I cared for and was driven to respond to their needs. Even though I knew I couldn't save the world, I had lived my life as if I could.

> *Even though I knew I couldn't save the world,*
> *I had lived my life as if I could.*

My drive took its toll. Like so many others in helping professions, I burned out. The early signs nudged me to move to a smaller town, take a job in a smaller organization, and get back to hands-on nursing care after several years as a public health bureaucrat. Within a couple years I was overwhelmed by the never-ending stream of pregnant teens and young women ill-equipped to deal with parenting, complicated by poverty, drug and alcohol abuse, or domestic violence. I battled to survive by moving into middle management. The impotence I felt in direct service was magnified in my new role caught between those with power and those in need. I finally realized that in response to overextending myself, I had withdrawn and nearly extinguished my compassion.

At the same time, my family felt squeezed by Middle America's compulsion to move faster, consume more, and question less. The treadmill was circling at a frantic pace, leaving us all gasping for breath and grabbing for a hand-hold. When I proposed a year in Stehekin to renew, their positive response was unanimous.

Despite my yearning for retreat, there was one concern I carried with me to Stehekin. As I moved to one of the most removed sites in our country, I feared I would forget. Forget the effects of abuse, disenfranchisement, and oppression. Forget injustice's aftermath if I no longer looked in the eyes of people who lived with it daily. Forget the despair of limited opportunities as I experienced the privilege of choosing a different way of life. In Stehekin, there would be no newspapers to link me to the rest of the world, no radio or TV newscasts. I couldn't call colleagues for updates about families I had worked with or responses to the latest communicable disease outbreak. The mountains that blocked the winter sun until mid-morning and swallowed it in the early afternoon kept me in the dark about events beyond my quiet refuge.

Our one-year sojourn turned into two. I hadn't expected that the boundaries of water and rock that divided me from others could restore a sense of communion but, nestled in the comforting arms of the valley, I regained awareness of my place in the circle of humanity. It wasn't the din of the media or the mass of case files that reminded me of my kinship with the earth and her creatures. It was my closeness to the beauty and power of nature that instructed my heart, rather than my head. My senses noticed interrelationships in different ways.

The gurgling of the Stehekin River told stories of its origins in the glaciers towering above me. Cycles of melting snows, rains, and droughts marked the passage of time in eroded river banks, sand bars, and jams of boulders and fallen, ancient trees. I saw clearly how the river's course was changed by eons of subtle events. Old growth ponderosa pines and Douglas firs reaching a hundred feet upward exalted the long history that preceded me, while new saplings following a forest fire were proof of future growth. Timid black bear cubs and spindly-legged fawns nibbling on plants sprouting through the melting spring snows just outside my door cued me to the mystery of new life.

There was no Quaker Meeting in Stehekin, so I went often to my favorite place of worship, a rock outcropping we named Boris's Bluff. It was Boris, our tabby cat, who showed me I didn't have to venture far behind our house to be deep in a wooded sanctuary. To my surprise, he always hiked along with me on my treks there. Together we walked through pine needles and scrambled over boulders that had rumbled down from mountain peaks over the centuries.

One day, sitting on a moss-covered rocky mound, I breathed in the pine scent of the surrounding woods and was warmed by the sun radiating off the stone. Encircled by mountain walls that gave the illusion there was nothing beyond, I was awed by an unexplainable feeling of connection with all people. It was in solitude, sitting alone on a rock, that I had a palpable awareness I wasn't alone. I realize now it was God's presence I experienced. Though I couldn't see or hear others, I felt their closeness and no longer feared I would forget. And I felt released from the responsibility to do it all; grasped it's not up to me alone.

Day after day, I could see the effect of the melting snows, the rush of the river, the delicate balance in nature, and they taught me that the smallest touch, the briefest contact, the quietest diligence, can make a difference—can change the course of a river. In the quiet safety of the forest and the mountains, I embraced both my smallness and my greatness.

I don't live in Stehekin anymore, but it lives in me. I didn't go back to the old house, or the old job. My family and I moved to a rural farming community on Lopez Island in Puget Sound. It has some of the best of Stehekin but is not so isolated. There's a grocery store, a high school, and a library. I figured out how to do only the parts of nursing I enjoyed the most and for several years shaped them into a private consulting practice. Eventually, I quit nursing all together and now work as a writer and artist.

My mainland friends presume that, as in Stehekin, island life is uncomplicated and comprised of long, contemplative hours. And it is, I suppose, in comparison to the pace and style of their lives. But even though we are still separated from that busier world by water and irregular ferry service, it often creeps in by phone, e-mail, and the Internet, and I can feel overwhelmed by the needs and struggles all around. So I continue to experiment with ways to preserve times of solitude, for I learned on Boris's Bluff that, for me, the silence is "the way through" to communion with God and the world.

Iris Graville

WILDNESS

QUERIES

Can you let go of the small "me" and experience the web of interrelationships in this world?

How do you listen for that which is beyond the smallness of your own concerns?

What nurtures your relationship with the Presence that animates this world?

BEACH MIST

Creating images in black and white forces the artist to consider perspective much more than creating in color, where the tones and hues of the scene bring familiarity and interest. Without color to create context and differentiation, I must consider other ways to convey the essence of the scene. Not unlike trying to discern Truth in a "murky" situation, I have to explore moving the camera to change spatial relationships. I watch the changes in the forms on the ground glass, trying to ignore the color and see just the relationships of shape, line and tone. I consider how the gray tones I see can be separated even more through filtration and/or altered film development. Often it's a kind of meditation. I remind myself, "Don't think too hard about it; watch, sense with more than just eyes. Have faith you'll know when it is right."

Chris Willard

SKYSTREAKING II

spring time night time
feeling them, then hearing
time stops, stands still
looking up to
geese on the move
in white shifting gentle lines
like smoke streaks
or those foamy lines that
receding tides leave on the beach

my Western Mind says
they are headed the wrong direction
because I still get north and east
mixed up in this place
and
they must be white
because they've caught
a light beam trapped under clouds
one
reaching out of Boise aways away

my Eastern Heart says
be still, be still
it's a gift
a blessing for you
breathe deeply

and then
they are gone

Sara Lee

SANGRE DE CRISTO

mountains meant for you, the bleed
and cleanse of apricot alpenglow
shed for you, behold the earth itself

poured out for you. Try again
to make yourself worthy of this
juniper, humbled at the gift

of piñon pine. There's only one hole
in this earth you could've
come from, and it's waiting

in the woodlands, carousing with the
grey fox kits, the badgers, with
the voles, it's holding spare

generations in its tunnels. Worship here
as reddened sandstone worships wind:
break me, move and make me as you please.

Maria Melendez

BRISTLECONE PINES

at ten thousand feet
in the White Mountains
cirrus clouds course
across a cerulean sky

wind screeching through canyons
racing across my face
unleashing my hair

in ages past
a Paiute elder sat beside this matriarch
let his breathe mingle with hers
touched his skin to hers

like him I am drawn to her
fingers stroke cinnamon ribbons of heartwood
arms embrace her serpentine trunk

grace seeps into me
transformed into nectar
that spills from my eyes
mends my heart

Charity Bryson

STILL VALLEY

Trying to continue some work I'd become engaged in, in hopes of prolonging a productive period I'd had the day before, and unable to find my way forward, I felt a need to go to the desert.

I picked up and got on a bus that took me, after a short ride, to that section of the mountainous nature preserve surrounding the city which I had begun to frequent. Approaching the peak I had come to think of as mine, by a path not tried before, I climbed up to the crest. Then I pressed on to a second, higher peak in the rough, stony, lonesome wilderness, surprised by the refreshment I felt and couldn't quite explain.

One moment particularly has stayed in my mind. Leaning on a bulk of rock—so sheer, smooth, sharp-edged, black shot through with red and rust, so dense, so weighty as if made of pure iron—I found it, in the shade, cold as ice, glacial. Laying my palm flat on it, my cheek daringly against it, letting the hot sun burn on my back —what peculiar pleasure. What deep respect I felt in the presence of this bold contrast, an unmitigated assertion of something being the way it is, with or without my understanding. I realized it was what I needed: to be lifted off into that which is beyond my control, knowing, anew, there is that. Going "outside of my head."

Descending on the other side of the range, I headed toward a little mountain pass that had really been the vision in my mind when I felt the drawing to the desert. Just a round dip in the crest between two mountains. When you climb up to it—just a short climb from the trail—you see nothing but its edge against the blue sky, you see nothing beyond it, and for all you know, the world breaks off there, and you can't imagine the nothingness beyond. But you climb, you trust, in joyous anticipation and also some primal fear, a fear that remains in us humans no matter how knowledgeable we get about the natural world. Your heart beats a little faster, and all your being gathers in a single focus. Who knows, beyond that rim perhaps the world will really be taken away. It is fitting that all your attention should come together for this.

And then, just before you reach the rim, another mountain peak appears beyond, in the distance, and now you are up—and the "beyond" opens to your eyes as a broad, lovely valley, like a wide, mild lap where your soul may find a moment's rest.

I call it the "still valley." This is because the mountains enclosing it block out the noise of the world (except for the occasional airplane overhead), from the freeway beyond the mountain to my right, to the east, with its steady stream of fast traffic. As I sit down in the light shade of the paloverde tree just to the right of the pass, facing the valley, I'm hearing the desert wind. A small wind that has suddenly gained a voice.

Your heart beats a little faster, and all your being gathers in a single focus. Who knows, beyond that rim perhaps the world will really be taken away. It is fitting that all your attention should come together for this.

I listen gratefully.

All natural things, all phenomena of the outward world, carry symbolic meaning for us humans. They teach us constantly about the deeper meaning of the things of life, the meaning they *really* have for us, though most of the time we are not aware of this reading.

During this hike, the ancient story of the prophet Elijah's long walk from Mount Carmel to Mount Horeb, the "mountain of God," and his experience there, had been in the back of my mind (1 Kings 19.) The story contains an episode characterized by the little phrase much beloved by Quakers: "the still, small voice." In heeding the desert wind's little voice now, the truth of that mythic experience opened further to me, with some greater depth than before. I felt how it is true—I hadn't always been so convinced—that God is not in the storm, not in the earthquake, not in the fire—but in the "sheer silence" of which the desert wind was only helping me to be aware.

I thought of the troubles in our world, all the things it is supposed to be bogged down with at this time, of which we constantly hear. And how I, too, in my little life, bump into this trouble, in- and outside of myself.

What is the reality of this stillness, I asked, this wholesomeness presently filling my field of vision, including me in itself, amidst all this trouble? And what is its weight? Is it irrelevant? Does it have meaning? Why do I seek it? And why is it nourishing—even restoring?

And in the wind's quiet whisper, the Elijah story said this to me:

God is not in our troubles, the storms, earthquakes, fires of our experience, though these come before Him and perhaps are signs preparing His way. We must let them pass, that God may pass before us: in the stillness that lasts through all the troubles, sustained and sustaining.

A concern of my Yearly Meeting was on my heart, that we may corporately discern God's will for us at this time. We had planned a special gathering in hopes that we may grow clearer about what is asked of us in the troubles of our age. I could not envision this gathering now other than as a time for us in the broad, still valley, of cool rock and bright, warm light, where we may hear the still, small voice of the "desert wind," the sound of God's silence in our hearts. The silence out of which Elijah, having brought his mighty complaint fully, honestly, and articulately before God and laid his soul bare in his helplessness, received the next inward command, the fresh "leading": his very own task in the Lord's work that it may be carried on in the world—as well as (here I felt my heart breaking) God's fresh, lasting promise that He would always leave "seven thousand"—the full number—in Israel whose knees will not bend before the Baal.

I felt with clarity how we need both these things. The fresh leading for action of which we feel desperately in need, rising out of this giving-up as we approach the rim of our vision beyond which the specter of our nothingness seems to await; and the fresh encouragement, God's own lasting promise renewed in our heart, a refreshing of our faith. And that we need to undertake this hike together, and this sitting in the valley.

Heidi Blocher

LISTENING TO ASPEN

On a recent fall trip to the Eastern Sierras, I reveled in a week of hiking among the aspen. Lining the trail, the trees formed an outdoor cathedral, resplendent with golden, orange, and lime light, vibrant as stained glass. White trunks led my eyes upwards to a cerulean dome. As on other trips in other times and other seasons, I felt in the presence of Spirit among these "Quaking aspen."

> *What is it about me that allows me to be moved? Is my stem my faith? The particular turning of my soul, my readiness to hear God's call, if I am still enough to listen?*

The leaves, like small, round Japanese fans, flickered and radiated yellow light. Looking toward the sun, the colors intensified; with the sun at my back, the leaves paled by comparison, suddenly dull and wan. Like the leaves, I need to turn towards the Light in order to be at my best.

The Latin name for aspen is *populus tremuloides*. Aspen tremble, shake and quiver with the slightest breeze, not unlike the way I feel when Spirit moves through me. French trappers believed that the cross Jesus was crucified on was made from aspen wood and that is why the trees still tremble. They also sensed God in the presence of these trees.

Scientists explain the movement of aspen leaves this way: their long, flattened stems attach perpendicular to the leaf, unlike stems on most deciduous leaves. The angle enhances their fluttering and enables them respond to a barely discernable breeze. What is it about me that allows me to be moved? Is my stem my faith? The particular turning of my soul, my readiness to hear God's call if I am still enough to listen?

Aspen trees thrive in abundant light. A hardy breed, they live from sea level to up to 11,500 feet. After forest fires, aspen trees regenerate quickly in the burned areas. Their underground roots spread laterally more than 100 feet, producing suckers that develop into young trees. When my own roots in Meeting are broad and deep, when I feel personal caring among us, when my daily practice nourishes me, I too thrive in the Light, even when I am "burned out" by life's challenges.

In the Eastern Sierra, aspen trees endure six to eight dark months of snow and ice. Young trees bend under the weight of the snow. But they straighten up again, with a curvy detour in their trunks. With God's love, I also bow through the many seasons of my life. "When true simplicity is gained, to bow and to bend we shan't be ashamed," the song reminds me. Because aspen trees bend easily they are not commercially valuable, except to make particleboard and pulp. Their flexibility favors their survival, both in the mountains and also in our human world of diminishing timber resources.

Aspens play their role in God's world. Deer, elk and moose eat the leaves and twigs, birds nest and take cover in branches, and beaver cut aspen trunks for dams. After fall rains, downed leaves turn brown and soggy . The soil under aspen trees is especially rich since the litter decays rapidly, hosting new life in the spring.

The most widely distributed trees in North America, aspen trees have endured some abuse. Hikers and hunters have carved their initials and names in the white bark of the larger trees. Since the 1800's Basque sheepherders have cut their names and their lovers' names on aspen trees all over the western United States. I saw one tree, its white bark stretched thin around a large trunk, with the message "Jesus Loves" and a cross carved above that. But aspen trees are resilient. Their scars heal with time, the bark becoming gray and thickened over past cuts as the trunk expands. So I too experience the miracle of healing with time. The Spirit mends mind, soul and body in a gradual redemption after brokenness.

Though aspen are resilient, most start deteriorating by age sixty, earlier in some stands. But because of their special root reproduction, scientists can trace some living aspen groves in Utah to ancestors that lived in the Pliocene era, more than 1 million years ago.

On my trip, I took pictures incessantly, trying to capture the brilliance of aspen in canyons and on mountainsides. In a quiet moment on the last day, I realized that I could not catch, freeze, or possess the glory of these trees. I learned to let go, to surrender to God's will and rhythms. I sat in silence, warming in the late afternoon sun.

As the cold wind blew gold leaves past me, I knew that soon the aspen trees would bare their branches completely, ready to receive the first snows of winter. Mountain chickadees would hop from one gray branch to another to catch the last rays of tepid sun. The sad words from Frost's poem "Nothing Gold Can Stay," haunted me. I started to feel dejected about life's ephemeral nature. An inner voice answered, "Find gold in the present."

I will return to the mountains next summer, God willing, when the new green leaves will rattle and tremble in the quiet air. I will be reminded of the presence and mystery of Spirit. In the stillness and the Light, I will listen to the aspen again.

Kathy Barnhart

MOTHER NATURE, MY MOTHER, AND ME

I see myself as a child, elementary school age, standing on the sidewalk in front of my house, engrossed in a serious conversation with a playmate. She is Catholic, I am unchurched. I am arguing that Mother Nature is the same as God. I am so sure I am right. She is sure I am wrong. Something about the strength of the conviction made me remember this incident.

Years later when I would remember, I would be embarrassed. Of course I was wrong. How could I have held so firmly to a to a position that was so naïve and misguided? Now, reading Matthew Fox and learning about feminine spirituality, I remember this incident again and laughingly see I have gone full circle. Now I can agree with my childish view. Mother Nature is God, can be God, would be a better God than the male sky-god so many accept. And now I see, having more insight into the child I was, that my certainty of my position was probably born of the fact that Mother Nature was my God. I was speaking from experience.

I found the above in my journal, an entry from 1985. When I think of my spiritual journey, mostly I think of the distance covered: from being raised outside religious traditions, passing through Unitarianism, then discovering Quakerism in my early thirties. But when I went to write a spiritual autobiography to present to my meeting's adult discussion last winter, I started by writing "My spiritual home is out of doors," and came to realize that I should acknowledge and thank my mother for her role in my early spiritual development in a way I'd never recognized before.

My mother's prime connection to nature arose from the long summers spent each year at our beloved summer cabin in the Adirondacks. We practically lived out of doors, and as an only child, I had lots of time to daydream while playing on the rocks in the rapids, the sound of the water surrounding me. This was, I'm sure now, the nurturing ground for my childhood spirituality, about which I remember very little beyond the sidewalk argument about God and Mother Nature. But I remember stories my mother told and anecdotes involving her.

My mother talked about a scene in the movie, "Teahouse of the August Moon" when everyone drops everything at the teahouse on

Okinawa to go outside to watch the sunset. And the spirit in which they do it, reverently, as if it's an important, meaningful thing to do, coming from the center of their lives. This is what she saw missing in American culture, and yearned for: making nature and natural beauty a meaningful part of life.

I now see it as letting nature have a spiritual meaning. I remember a story that Conrad McEwen, an Adirondack woodsman/carpenter friend of my parents told my mother one summer when I was in my teens. One of his daughters had married a Catholic who liked to flaunt his religiousness to his parents-in-law who did not attend church. Finally McEwen said to him, "I am as religious as you are, but my church is the woods." This story stuck in my memory to take on meaning much later. He must have sensed it would be meaningful to my mother, who I'm sure felt the same way, but had never put it in those words. My mother died in 1976, but there was a time later when I wished I could run back and tell her that she was not alone, that now people spoke of connecting spirit with nature, and that the out-of-doors was central to my spiritual experience. She had thought she was so alone.

The message is now more widespread than in her day and appears in some surprising places. The visitors' center at North Cascades National Park in Washington State presents a hauntingly beautiful slideshow every half-hour entitled, "A Meditation of Wilderness." Stunning slides fade into each other with an audio background drawn from various sources, including Native American. At one point the narrator says, "Wilderness is the earth's temple. Worship here."

Susan Merrill

FAMILY
&
COMMUNITY

QUERIES

Are you open to the gifts of love and wisdom offered by friends and family?

How does your respect for that of God in every person help you care for others?

How does your awareness of the Light in all people empower you to create healthy and loving relationships? Does it help you accept the burdens, as well as the gifts, of relationships?

WADE IN THE WATER
An Underground Railroad Quilt

Susan D. Hopkins

The quilt began as a single block depicting the story and song, "Follow the Drinking Gourd" stitched in the appliquéd style modeled by Harriet Powers. It shows Peg Leg Joe leading the slaves out of the river to freedom guided by the Big Dipper and the North Star. The second appliquéd block was created using a parallel theme which showed Moses leading the People of Israel to freedom across the Red Sea, told in the story and song "Go Down Moses." The final title selected for the quilt, " Wade in the Water," was chosen to draw upon the courage, faith in God, and the pursuit of justice by so many over the years. "Wade in the Water" speaks to us of God's mercy as the waters of the Red Sea were parted and as the American rivers gave hope to those escaping bondage. God's gonna trouble the waters for yet a long time to come.

RETURN TO MOUNTAIN CAMP

The palms lead, release the flow.
Turn and turn again, let go.

Sell the crystal, give away
the white teapot with yellow flowers.
Toss the files marked "to read" (someday).
Keep the poems, the picture of your brother,
four years old on the dock by Odell Lake,
small, blond, alone. Keep the letters
from your father, echoes across a deep canyon.

Trucks come from Parents Anonymous
and Disabled American Veterans,
haul away the detritus of years.
High water floods the canyon,
scours the beaches clean.

Open the palms, breathe and release,
turn toward the Tiger's Mouth.
Rose window light. A vast space
and you in its center, centered.

Eleanor Dart

TIME ON MY HANDS

I draw the splayed hand, time ticking
at the wrist. Broad, peasant
fingers with stubby strength—
my first boyfriend held this brown
hand and called me "milkmaid."

My father's hands were blunt, too,
broader than the piano keys.
Time ticks on. Artist Grandma
Layton drew hands by contour
with all the lines and blemishes
etched without vanity. Praying hands
like steeples, and healing hands.
A pulse also ticks at the wrist.

Time is in the dough rising
after the kneading and waiting,
and in the choir director's hands
that slow the bass and lift the soprano.

We try to understand time
and can only say it is in God's hands.

Judy Ray

THIRD GENERATION

I am the third generation of my memory.
I hear the voices of the two before
encircle within my arms the next two
with luck will know the one following
and
imagine in my sweet dreams the final of the string.

If I think of myself as the first generation
then the embracing of the next two
leaves five for the heartholding.

I can put them all into a timeframe that I understand.
These generations are as real to me as my own breath.
These generations are not only mine... they belong to the world.
They and all of the other living beings
and
all of the things that now exist or have or will
these everyday everythings that carry the spirit of creation
through simply being,
these all together are The World.

Just as we know our own flesh and blood and understandings
just as we must take care of each other
so we must cherish and care for our Sacred Mother Earth
for She is us and we are Her.

Sara Lee

LIVING PEACEFULLY

Sleeping on my lap
        our bodies conforming to each other
        she is without trepidation
        safe in the world
            warm and cozy she reminds me
            to live without fear

Sitting in her high chair
        sometimes standing
        she is excited by life
        fed by the world
            her full belly reminds me
            to trust

Playing in our living room
        exploring with toys
        she learns
        the ways of the world
            engaging her mind she reminds me
            I am safe

Greeting others outside our home
        with a wave and a kiss
        she is curiously
        greeting the world
            interacting with others she reminds me
            to reach out to community

God has blessed me twice
        once by her presence
        again with a model to live peaceably

Darlene Colborn

PRAYER

In the darkness of the night,
I awake to the memories
Of sad thoughts.
But sad thoughts fade
When I think of all those
Who pray for me.

I think of you:
With your wild wacky humor,
Hanging me out to dry in God's Wind.
I remember you:
With your quiet grace,
Lifting me up into God's Care.
I cherish you:
With your gentle message,
That holds my heart steady in Love.
I thank you:
With your bear hug arms,
Holding me close in the Light.
I bless you:
With your generous heart,
That sends waves of God's Presence
Flowing into my life.

Then I realize
That You, Oh Divine One,
Are praying for me
In the hearts of these dear Friends.
Your Care reaches out to me
Through them,
As You enfold each one of us
In Your Meditation of Love.

Mary Miche

ONE CHILD'S SHOE

In June of 1942 my father, Francis Dart, and my mother, Alice Adams, were married. They honeymooned in a secluded cottage on Lake Michigan. "We were so happy," my mother wrote. "But underneath we knew the world was tearing apart. Talking it all over we became aware that we both wanted to be among those who 'live in the Life and Power that takes away the occasion for wars.' We pledged to God and to each other that if Francis was allowed to get his Ph.D. without interruption we would offer two years of his life to the American Friends Service Committee."

And so in January of 1947, just two months after I was born, my father went to German as a Quaker Relief worker. He was thirty-three years old. His experiences there changed his life, and affected our family in powerful ways. When he came back I was just over two years old, and my sister Helen was three and a half. He used to tell us stories about things he'd seen in those years, to teach us about love and suffering, and the good that can be touched in every human heart.

When World War II ended, German-speaking people who had lived for generations in Poland, Czechoslovakia, Hungary and all over Eastern Europe were uprooted, put on trains, and sent to war-ravaged Germany. Farmers, teachers, shopkeepers, housewives, children— millions of people were systematically moved out of their homes, and sent west. My father wrote, "They were allowed to take no money, no belongings except what they could carry with them. They did not know where they were going, indeed no one knew until they were put of the transport according to an arbitrary distribution. They found themselves in a strange town without funds or resources. They did not want to come, and they were not wanted."

These were the refugees, the *Fluchtlinge*. In the town of Oldenburg, where my father was posted, a team of ten Quakers did what they could to help. There were shortages—or total lack—of everything: shelter, heat, blankets, food medicine, clothing, shoes.

One of the refugees who got off the train in Oldenburg was a shoemaker. He made his way to the Quaker center and offered his services. But there was no leather to be had. Oldenburg was in the

American Zone, and a U.S. Army Depot was located there, to supply military troops. Most of the troops had already been demobilized and gone home. My father went to the Army Depot and met with a young man who was the Quartermaster.

This U.S. soldier sat behind a shiny desk. On the desk was a picture of his wife and small son. My father told him about his two young daughters, and they talked for a while about their families, so far away.

"Are there any leather goods in the depot?" my father asked. They walked through the storage rooms and found stacks and stacks of leather holsters for Army issue revolvers. "Would it be possible for you to let us have some of these for making shoes?" my father asked.

"No, no, it's against regulations; it can't be done," was the Quartermaster's reply.

"Well, could I perhaps have just one holster?"

"Sure, why not? Who would miss it?" he said

So he gave my father one leather holster and said goodbye. My father went back to the Quaker center and gave the holster to the shoemaker. Three days later the shoemaker brought back a single small child's shoe. "U.S. Army" it read, across the toe.

My father took the shoe to the Army Depot and asked to speak again with the young Quartermaster. He put the single child's shoe on the desk. The Quartermaster looked at it for a long time without speaking.

"You can have all the leather you can use," he said.

What can one person do, in the face of immense suffering? I believe, as my father taught me through his stories, that all the help in the world comes from individuals who open their hearts, one person at a time.

Eleanor Dart

STEMMING THE FLOOD

I stood wet and naked, under a window open to a cold November breeze, in an unfamiliar shower stall. I was trying to get the cold water tap to turn off. It didn't turn off in the usual direction; I turned it the other way and the force of full-on cold water blew the faucet off in my hand. A geyser of icy water smashed into the opposite shower wall and over me.

There was no plumbing turn-off valve visible. Desperately I tried to force the faucet handle over the flood. I was trying to seat it so that I could at least turn down the flow. As I pushed with all my strength the handle forced the water to squirt out the sides, flooding into the small changing room as well. An image flashed into my mind: the Dutch boy with his thumb in the hole in the dike. Like the boy, I felt that I couldn't give up my effort to stem the flood—disaster would result! Perhaps a passerby saw the boy and called for help; who would find me? It was Thanksgiving Day and most residents of the mobile home/RV park were gone. I was the only one using the bath house.

Finally I gave up and moved myself into the adjoining wash room. I almost wrapped my damp towel around me and ran out into the cold to try to find someone to help. I was ready to brave the cold, and strangers, naked and wet to try to stop the flood!

Suddenly everything shifted. It was as though someone put a hand on my shoulder, calming me. "Get dressed! Get warm first before you seek help," was the message given to me. It was more than just a message of action to take: it was a palpable inner reminder that I was more important than this emergency. First I needed to care for myself—wet, shivering and in shock.

I dressed hurriedly, went outside and called. A large young man appeared from a nearby mobile home. He was so calm; his calm was a steadying balm to me. I showed him the situation. "I'll get Pedro," he said. No panic, such as mine. Just efficient action. The two men took on the project and I was freed to walk back to our trailer home.

As I walked, I received a message, with laughter, from my inner guides. "It's the story of your life!" they told me. "Taking responsibility for something that goes wrong, that you can't fix, and doggedly trying to make it right irregardless of the cost to you!"

Dan and I discussed this. Why did I stay in the cold water so long, futilely trying to put the handle back on? Why was I even willing to run into the cold, towel-wrapped and shivering, to look for help?

"I was wasting all that water!" I told him. It was then apparent to me that because I'd been holding the knob when it came off, I felt responsible for its breakage. As the one "responsible" for the disaster, I needed to fix it! Even when my fix-it efforts weren't working.

My partner Dan helped me to identify old operating patterns in this event: guilt by association, a sense of responsibility to fix whatever goes wrong; a willingness to sacrifice myself in this effort, even if it's not within my competence to change it for the better.

I questioned the base of these patterns more deeply. Do I believe that no help is available except what I can provide? That there is no one better able to solve the problem than I am? Do I expect to sacrifice myself for every worthy cause that I happen upon?

What has impacted me most in this experience is that help came to me for myself, even when I hadn't asked for this. What an enormous shift it will be for me—and for all of us!—when we realize that we are precious: *we* are the Beloveds.

Sometimes help comes to us unexpectedly. It helps to stop our futile actions long enough to realize what is offered! Sometimes we have to ask. Asking for help to solve problems, whether seemingly personal or societal ones, builds community. Focused community efforts can resolve even seemingly impossible problems. Supporting each other in community, we become extensions of the greater Love that supports us all.

Now, if I can only remember all this the next time a faucet handle blows off in my hands!

Alicia Adams

THE HOLIDAY VISITOR

My grandmother's annual holiday visit was fraught with tension. Grandma stayed in my room, displacing me to the couch, where I had no privacy, no retreat for daydreaming and imagining and pondering. She poked through my things and found them wanting. In fact, nothing was ever good enough for the diminutive family matriarch.

We took her to the best restaurant in town, where she clucked and spluttered over the prices. After we had been served, she sent back the clam chowder she had ordered, telling the waiter, "Young man, please tell the chef I ordered soup, not wallpaper paste."

I invited her to watch us practice for the school play ("Your grandmother would love to see what you're working on," my mother told me—which was mother-speak for, "Please take her out of my hair for a while.") I thought we were stunning. Hollywood-material, even.

"All I saw was a lot of fooling around and giggling," Grandma said.

"Play Scrabble with your grandmother," Dad said, and so we did, and when my sister made up a word (fangipaz), I laughed.

"That's all well and good," Grandma said, pursing her lips, "if you want her to grow up to be a cheater."

Grandma often brought her enormous cat, Max. Sometimes, Max would curl up on the nearest available lap, and consent to be petted; other times, acting out of some inexplicable feline malice, he would bite. Hard.

Of course, Grandma also made the best gingersnaps in the known universe. And she brought interesting photographs of the places she had visited. If we behaved ourselves—if we said thank you for the cookies and refrained from swearing at Max— there would be an invitation to join her on the next trip.

When I was seventeen, supremely conscious of my role as the center of all things, I decided I had had enough. I was going to stop trying to please That Woman. I would just accept the fact that my grandmother was impossible, that she would never be pleased with me, and that, if Max was ever gracious enough to die, he'd simply come back again as a spiteful ghost.

That was when I noticed, for the first time, that Grandma grimaced in pain when she was getting ready to stand up or sit down.

And that Grandma always took our side in an argument with our parents ("They've got to grow up sometime," she'd say).

And that she took every opportunity to tell anyone who would listen how proud she was of her grandchildren (she once mortified me by writing a letter to the editor of the local newspaper, mentioning me by name, demanding to know why they didn't print more stories about good people, people like her granddaughter who was a straight-A student).

That was the year—perhaps he recognized some sign of readiness—that my father explained our family history to me. Grandma's husband was an alcoholic, he told me, who had abandoned his family when my father and his brother were very young. Grandma raised her sons alone, at a time when society did not provide many opportunities for financial independence for any woman, let alone a single mother.

Grandma raised her sons alone, at a time when society did not provide many opportunities for financial independence for any woman, let alone a single mother.

Hearing her story, I wondered how my grandmother managed to save enough to take me, my sister, and my cousins traveling. Nanoseconds later, I understood in a flash of painful clarity the reason for her annoying habit of bringing only two pairs of underwear (wear one, wash the other in the sink and hang it out to dry, usually where a grandchild would have to endure the humiliating agony of running into the drying undergarment at least once), forcing us to eat every last crumb of every meal, and rejecting suggestions that we see a Broadway musical or visit a famous (expensive) restaurant.

During Christmas Eve services, I sat close to Grandma, and rested my head on her shoulder. Her voice, warbling the carols, resonated through her fragile shoulder bones into my ear. The flickering candlelight shone on the lines of her skin—each line a mark of some experience, she liked to say, good or bad, all proof of a life well-lived.

As we sat together, I began to understand perhaps for the first time the meaning of love demonstrated rather than spoken, the kind of love that goes without so that others may have, the kind of love that gave its only son to an unseeing world. And there on the hard, cold church pew, that of God in my grandmother—critical and persnickety though she most certainly was—moved me so that I could say, if only for a moment, I was blind, but now I see.

Shari Lane

PARABLES & FABLES

QUERIES

Stories are ways we understand some portion of the Truth. What is a story—truth or fiction—that sings to you?

When have you started something on faith not knowing how way would open?

Who are you? What keeps you from being yourself?

LISTENING PRAYER

from the "Fables" series

My "Fables" series of paintings represent my struggle in coming to terms with my spiritual side. Each is directly inspired by the Bible Study sessions at my Meeting, where we have been reading the Scripture from beginning to end for the last three years.

Biliana Stremska

PAY ATTENTION

Meg paused on the stoop before stepping onto the brick-red walkway that led out to the sidewalk. The day's blue sky eased into black. Across the street, the almost-full moon glowed through the leaves of the oak trees fronting the neighbor's tangled yard. A mourning dove, or perhaps an owl, hooted into the dusk. To her left, at the edge of the yard, white bursts of jasmine grew into the juniper bush. She thought she might pull the vines, after the blooms were spent.

Meg's dog, Wonder, a 100-pound bear of an animal, limped slowly and deliberately, favoring his right front leg. A recent x-ray had revealed cancer: a tumor cratered and pitted the dog's ankle joint, removing bone mass. Soon, there would be no bone left and Wonder's leg would snap.

At most, Wonder could walk just two blocks—one block in each direction. The foray took them a good twenty minutes. Without fail, Wonder would stop and sniff the telephone pole in front of Meg's small stucco house, the clump of poppies in the front yard three houses down, the heap of weed-infested red lava rocks at the fifth house, and the stretch of wood chips along the edge of the sidewalk by their turn-around spot. Meg admired Wonder's faithfulness. He'd sniffed at the same patches for weeks now. Was this habit, or research? Did he catch something new each time, an odor that had previously escaped him?

Meg wished she could be so faithful. To anything. Several months ago, she tried to add a fifteen minute meditation to her daily routine, but that time had been shoved out of her schedule by more pressing demands: her family, her work as a first-grade teacher, the housework, her sporadic exercise routine. And the last time she attended Meeting for Worship had been at least three weeks ago. As a casual attender, she appreciated the silence, more for the absence of noise than for the notion that the Spirit, the ethereal Light, existed in everyone and could speak directly to anyone, anytime. That thought still overwhelmed her, implying a responsibility she wasn't sure she could shoulder.

At the corner, Meg gently tugged on Wonder's leash. But the dog kept his head down, sniffing the bush he'd sniffed countless times before. His lips trembled and a line of drool snaked from his mouth.

Meg thought about the last time she'd been to Meeting for Worship. It had been a large gathering, maybe sixty people or more. After the fifth speaker, Meg had imagined escaping the worship room and sinking into a comfy chair in the library across the hall. Instead, she remained.

Just as she'd regained her silence, she heard the telltale shifting and the creak of shoes as someone stood. She glanced up and tensed. Charles. Every time that man spoke, Meg tuned out. He offered lengthy ministry on anything Biblical, from the Old Testament to the New.

But today, Charles did something different. He did not speak. With a quick glance, Meg saw that he was shifting his weight from leg to leg, as if he were nervous, a condition she'd never attribute to him. Charles sported a mantle of humbleness, which Meg suspected cloaked a severe arrogance and a critical character. She'd spoken to him only once, when she bumped into him on her way out of the worship room. They'd exchanged pleasantries.

Charles still stood. Meg could sense a tension in the room, as if the collective also wondered what Charles was up to. Another minute passed, then two. Three. Would someone from the Ministry & Oversight committee stand with him? Someone weighty who would knew what to do?

Just as she'd regained her silence, she heard the telltale shifting and the creak of shoes as someone stood. She glanced up and tensed. Charles.

Finally, Charles spoke, uttering just two words: "Pay attention." He sat down. No sermon, no lecture, no booming oratory. Just those two simple words.

That was the last message Meg heard.

"Pay attention pay attention pay attention." The mantra floated through her, easing her own rambling thoughts. A curious gratitude, followed by a warm glow, sunk into her. She was so lost her in her silence that she startled when the person next to her touched her on the shoulder and grasped her hand. The hour was already over? What

97

had happened? After the worship room emptied, Meg continued to sit. What did the phrase "pay attention" really mean? And why had those two small words resonated with her, today? Without thought, without paying attention, she'd repeated those words countless times to her own children and to the multitudes of children who'd passed through her classroom.

Now, as she absently watched Wonder, Meg shook her head, remembering her clarity on that day. Sitting in the worship room, she'd promised to live by that mantra. She would meditate on that mantra, daily. She would pay attention. Well, here it was, at least a month later and she hadn't given it another thought. She hadn't paid attention any more than usual.

Meg sighed. Another resolution tossed. Wonder glanced up at her. Wonder could pay attention, Meg thought. His life had been one of attentiveness, of a keen and immediate awareness of what was right before him: food, an unusual smell, a cat, the need to sleep. He'd been attentive to her, to her moods, to her presence and absence. He wasted no energy on future expectations or past regrets.

When they reached the house, Wonder stopped in front of the stoop. Meg stepped up, opened the door, and called him. "Come on, Wonder." Wonder panted. He looked at her, then glanced down, then looked back up at Meg.

"Wonder, it's time to come in," Meg repeated. Wonder refused, planting his feet and locking his knees. Meg crouched in the doorway and extended her hand. "Come on in," she repeated. The dog would not budge.

As she thought about what treat she could use for a bribe, Meg glanced down. A six-inch long golden salamander rested on the stoop, barely visible against the red tiles. It was a miracle she hadn't stepped on it.

Meg stared. Then, she opened the front door, picked up a magazine from the day's mail, and gently prodded the salamander onto the slick paper. As she lifted it to eye level, the creature took a few steps. Its body curved like a snake and left a trail of slime on the paper. Meg carefully walked to the side of the house and placed the magazine at the base of a shrub. Within seconds, the salamander disappeared.

Meg sat down on the grass. "Pay attention pay attention pay attention," Meg thought. Wonder limped over and pushed his head against her hand. "Pay attention." Meg patted Wonder's head and put her arms around his neck. Suddenly, the same warmth that had flooded her during Meeting for Worship visited her again.

"Pay attention."

Meg lifted her head, keeping her arm around Wonder's shoulder, relishing his soft fur. A slight breeze, warm against her cheeks, rustled the fronds on the palm in her front yard. The shadows, cast by moon, seemed to wave at her. Catching a whiff of jasmine floating on the breeze, she breathed deeply and waited—expectant and open.

Nancy Wood

SUPERNOVA WITHIN

I call 1979 my "supernova year." It started inauspiciously. Self-doubt afflicted me as I realized I was far from accomplishing goals I once had. I was suffering from a confusion of obligations, to my family with adolescent boys, to community, to my aging parents, and to my gift of art.

In February of that year, I began going to the home of Alan and Joanne Strain on first Sundays. For several years, they had been holding informal Meetings for Worship every month in their woodland home. Often we met on a beautiful veranda under redwood trees. The small group had an intimacy I had not experienced in the large Palo Alto Meeting—indeed, not since high school workcamp worship.

At the time I joined the group, Joanne's breast cancer, dormant for years, had metastasized to her bones. She was 53, only ten years older than myself. Her oncologist decided to remove her ovaries. "I'd like to watch," she said, and they let her. I was shaken by her courage and knowledge of my own mortality. What were my unrealized dreams? What were Joanne's dreams, ones that never would be realized?

I experienced deep questions and yearnings. I remembered the teachers at my high school, Westtown Friends, who had shared their spiritual awakenings. I realized in my senior year that I had not mastered all Westtown had to teach me, that there was something more. What was that "something more" that *they* had found? If we were supposed to feel God's presence at Friends Meeting, what was it, and why didn't I feel it?

In the midst of my malaise, a friend made a casual remark about a free course at a local hospital that had helped her get her life together. Intuitively, I knew I needed it. The teacher, Elad Levinson, was funny and engaging, but also deeply serious. He had struggled with the addiction called obesity, and taught other kinds of addicts being treated at the hospital what he had learned. Then, he opened the class to anyone, for the life skills he taught were really about coping with the human condition. The only price of admission was that we come regularly and be on time.

Elad also occasionally held weekend retreats called Enlightenment Intensives, based on the work of Charles Berner in 1968. It struck Berner that the task of "enlightenment" is getting past your false self-image to a knowledge of your inner truth. There was no incompatibility with Quakerism, for this is also the aim of Friends' worship, but he conceived a disciplined, focused way to accelerate the process by a three-day retreat, which he honed over several years and taught to others.

Elad organized an Enlightenment Intensive at low cost in a small home in the hills of Redwood City. It wasn't, and still isn't, well-known, so I was in the dark about it, but I trusted him. There were a dozen of us. It was a cohesive group: many already knew each other from the class.

The retreat involved sitting meditation and walking meditation, listening and being listened to, and some astute guidance from Elad. We divided into pairs. Each time, the partner would ask, "Tell me who you are," and listen without comment for 20 minutes. Then, we would exchange places, and be the listener. The next session would be with a new partner. One thing we were instructed to do was to look steadily in people's eyes as we talked and listened. How seldom are we given permission to do this! Done for hours on end, it resurrects memories of looking at Mother. With a safe place to voice our inner thoughts, surprising things surfaced.

By the third day, I felt at odds with the elation that others in the room were obviously feeling. As I put it at the time, it was "like a person locked out of her car looking inside at the keys." Elad advised some of us that what was holding us back was the need to forgive.

He then spent some private time with each of us. I told him, "I have no one I feel badly towards... except, perhaps, myself."

" For what?"

"For not being multilingual or being a traveler, for not doing good in the world like a social worker, but also for not being more visible in the art world—yet at the same time being a great mom."

When all this came tearfully bubbling out of me, and we both looked at it, we had to laugh! A burden lifted!

The good teacher said to the group, "Some of you are so close, but not entirely there!"

I came up privately and asked what he meant. He put a hand on the back of my head and said, "Now do you feel it?"A sudden, visceral warmth spread over me, a sensation of light. As I stood at the wide windows that overlooked the bay and glow of the setting sun on the East Bay hills thirty miles away, the room and all of us in it were one. Inside and outside were one. We were invisibly but palpably radiant.

I call this my "supernova," because the radiance lasted a long time, and released reservoirs of psychic energy. Looking back on my life, I saw similar episodes of great exertion followed by elation, most notably, natural childbirth. It seemed as if they were beads on a string, leading me to this point and giving the direction of the way forward.

For days afterwards, I bicycled around town fervently singing "Amazing Grace."

"Nevertheless, it will fade," said my older artist friend, Edith Smith, who had spontaneously experienced something very similar. "It's like being in love in that way." It did, yet like a supernova, it left valuable residues. The cosmic event leaves heavy elements, which make life possible. The psychic one, an aftermath of joy, discipline and courage. In effect, it was like a conversion experience, in that it led to greater resoluteness and direction in my life. I became serious about my practice, about compassion, and my commitment to the Friends Meeting community.

It is rare. I feel blessed to have experienced it. In my immaturity, I hoped for another episode, but this didn't happen. (Neither did it recur for Mother Teresa, who experienced illumination on a railroad journey as a young woman, the experience that set the course of her life. She said she spent the rest of her life looking for it.)

I had a chance before Joanne died to share with her the path she had unwittingly sent me on, and to tell her she was my mentor.

Trudy Myrrh Reagan

WHY ARE THERE STARS?

This is a story of the young man who earnestly sought true knowledge of God. He had left his home and traveled through a deep forest to study with a teacher who lived in a cave under a hill.

After he had been studying for some time, the young man went to his teacher and said, "I want clear answers about why things are the way they are. Why did God make the world as it is?" He paused to think of an example, then asked, "Why are there stars in the sky?"

The wise woman answered by saying, "I am not wise enough to answer that question. Perhaps you should go into the village in the valley and ask people there."

The young man walked down the hill to the village and along its dusty main street. The first person he saw was the blacksmith, working in the smithy by the millpond. He asked the blacksmith, "Why are there stars in the sky?"

"Why, everybody knows that!" exclaimed the smith, setting down his hammer. "The stars are sparks from the war gods in the heavens sharpening their swords and spears. I'll show you; just start turning the handle on this grindstone."

The young man turned the handle and the stone spun on its axle. The smith took a pair of pruning shears and held one blade to the stone. Sparks flew from the edge of the blade where it touched the wheel.

"The sparks are droplets of molten iron," said the smith. "The hardest steel makes the longest lasting sparks. The stars seem to us to be fixed in the sky because the war gods' blades are steel so hard the sparks last for an age. If you ever see the stars stop shining, beware! The war gods have finished sharpening their weapons and are ready to do battle!"

The young man thanked the blacksmith, and walked on along the street. The next person he came to was an old man with a fishing pole, sitting on the bank of the millpond. He asked the fisherman, "Why are there stars in the sky?"

"Why, everybody knows that!" exclaimed the old man, raising his fishing pole to see if he had a bite. "You see that big fish jumping out there, just past the reach of my line? See how the spray shines in the sun when he splashes back into the pond? The stars are drops of water splashed into the sky when a really, really big fish jumps. They seem to us to be fixed in the sky because it is such a big fish that the splash lasts for an age. If you ever see the stars stop shining, it means the fish has gone down deep to get up speed for another jump!"

The young man thanked the fisherman, and turned toward the path up the hill. He passed a farmhouse at the edge of town, where in the yard a woman was milking a goat. He asked her, "Why are there stars in the sky?"

"Why, everybody knows that!" she exclaimed. "A great goddess who lives in the heavens is milking her goat, just as I am milking mine. The stars are drops of goat's milk that splash out of her bucket. There are so many stars because the goddess has an enormous bucket, as big as the sky! If you ever see the stars stop shining, it means the goddess has enough milk to start making cheese."

The young man thanked the farmwife, and continued up the hill to his teacher's cave. He said to her when he arrived, "All I heard in the village were three superstitious stories about how the stars are droplets in the sky. Nobody said anything about why there are stars."

"What do your books say about how the stars came to be?" asked the wise woman, sliding the shuttle through the warp of her loom.

"That at the time of the Big Bang, all the matter and energy in the Universe exploded outward in a huge splash. Some of the matter condensed into drops big enough to ignite and become stars."

"So now you have four stories about how the stars came to be. What do they have in common, besides splashes?"

"In none of the stories is there any intention to make stars at all! They just happened while the war gods, or the fish, or the goddess, or God was doing something else. That can't be true!"

As she turned back to her loom, his teacher said, "If we admit that no one knows the truth of God's intention, then we have a choice of how we answer. Wouldn't you prefer the answer to be a story?"

Eric E. Sabelman

Father Abraham was getting old, and although he was loath to admit it to himself, he knew that soon it would be his time. But until then, he still had work to do.

Considering the relationship they had developed over the years, God decided that He wasn't simply going to send the sickle of death to cut Father Abraham down. Rather, He called upon Archangel Michael, and told him to convince Father Abraham that the time had come and to ascend with him. "Do not take him until he is ready," He said, "Make sure he has tied up all his loose ends."

Michael came down and told Father Abraham why he had come. "Not now," replied Father Abraham," dismissing him with a wave of the hand and then wiping the sweat from his furrowed brow. He leaned heavily into his plow, the ox pulling it forward straining at the reins. "I still have this field to sow. Otherwise my people will have to do without the spring harvest."

Michael shook his head. "All right," he said, "I'll come back later."

In spring, he returned. "Not now," said Father Abraham, shaking his wispy white beard, his spotted hands covered in blood. "It is birthing season for the sheep, and I must help them through it."

Michael protested for a moment, but seeing as it was useless, he said he'd come back later.

He came back in the fall. "Not now," said Father Abraham, filling his apron with red ripe pomegranates picked from the trees he had long ago planted along the riverbanks. "It is time to harvest what we have worked so hard to plant, and with which the Lord has blessed us."

Michael returned in winter. The harvest was in. The sheep grazed lazily on the hillsides. The plowing and sowing yet awaited. "It's time," said Michael, awaiting the expected reply.

"Let's go for a little walk," said Father Abraham, taking up his staff and throwing his old cloak over his left shoulder.

Together they climbed to the tops of the hills whereby they could peer down into the neighboring villages.

"See there," said Father Abraham, pointing to a village of ramshackle huts, "The harvest has failed, and we must go down and feed them."

They walked on and looked down into another valley, from where they heard a loud wailing. "There are many people there who are sick with fever. We must go down and heal them."

On they went. Down in the next valley, all they could hear was a rasp of metal against whetstone, as the men sharpened their daggers and spears, the women and children crouching fearfully by themselves at a safe distance. "They are preparing for war," said Father Abraham, "We must go down and teach them another way."

They walked on. The sun was setting, and an angry red sky reflected down into the last valley, from which they heard the muffled keening of women, and an occasional child's cry. And on the ground, beside several open pits, wrapped in white cloth from head to foot, were several bodies prepared for burial. "We must go down and comfort them, and let them know that in the face of death, there is always new life springing."

"There is so much left to do," said Father Abraham, returning home.

"That there is," said Michael. He scratched his head, confused, and flew off to consult further with the Most High as to what to do next.

The next season, as Father Abraham set to plowing again, Michael returned. "The Lord has commanded me to bring you a blessing," he said, and, putting his outstreteched hands on Father Abraham's shoulders, continued, "Blessed are you, for you have fulfilled the purpose for which you were sent."

At that, and hearing the truth winging into new ears, Father Abraham sat down on the half-plowed earth. And there they struck an agreement. Father Abraham ascended with the Archangel Michael, and from that day forth out of the corners of heaven, he has looked down upon the generations of men and blessed those that would feed the poor, heal the sick, seek peace in the world, and console the living, fulfilling the purposes for which we have been sent.

David H. Albert

CREATION MYTH FOR THE NEW CENTURY

One day God had a strawberry soda for lunch. After he had sucked up the last drops from the bottom of the glass, he playfully blew his breath through the straw.

At least, that is all he had intended.

But out of the end of that straw came a tremendous blast of energy. You and I call that the Big Bang, and it was the beginning of ever-widening sweeps of energy that never end. Hydrogen and helium emerged, then other elements, and matter formed. There were vast galaxies, and among them our little sun and planetary system.

Inanimate materials became sensitive to light and temperature; formerly inert matter began to react to the new situation. These animated cells somehow organized themselves to multiply. And pretty soon there were bacteria, and plants, and fish, and animals. Life forms of an amazing variety and complexity developed, living both within and opon each other.

Among the mammals, compassion grew out of our need for one another—and irritation, too! Ideas and concepts came into being. We humans began to think, and we tried to *think about our thinking*, and the resultant feedback raised fearful howls around the world.

In God's little puff of breath out of that straw came all the possibilities that were and are to be in the unfolding process of the universe. We live in, and are a part of, that continuing creation. There is yet a destiny far beyond our comprehension, of an ever-expanding universe of sensitivities, subtleties, and awareness that we cannot even imagine.

Don Elton Smith

CREATIVITY

QUERIES

How are various modes of expression, such as music, movement, or art, avenues of sharing experiences of the Divine for you?

In what "things" have you sensed the Holy Spirit?

How do you demonstrate your respect for life?

QALB (Allah Heart)

Through contact with Turkish culture, where Ebru art evolved, I gained an appreciation of the sacredness of the names and forms elaborated within the calligraphic arts of Islamic tradition. These names encompass sacred attributes that lead the one who utters or beholds them to a place that is beyond any word. This work is an act of worship, and allows me to express something beyond language.

Reza Antoszewska

MAILBAG

The poet is witness, and
  messenger too I suppose. Carrying about awkward
 bundles of words and thought fragments.
        thread ends of metaphors
 like a peddlar or the postman, drawing out
        of the backpack, the mailbag, pulling out of the deep pool
 messages from God, maybe your message, some word... You are
        waiting, you do not know it, for the right hand of Light
to grab you by your scruff and thrust whatever
 the meaning is,
  in your face, battering your nose with the
 rumpled envelope—*See! Here!*
  (Or is it: *Hear!* yes, it is, just listen),
 astonished eyes and all. In the cathedral
  of your heart the litany of praise
        and thanksgiving goes on day and night
—mostly you do not hear it, perhaps you are in
The Temple of If Only—it's right next door
        or maybe across the street at
        The Shrine of Oh Well... You forget
to remember the ark of gratitude. It sinks
 into the piles of unfolded laundry, is buried
 by the shopping list, until some fuzzy afternoon or weary
  evening the lizard of happiness crawls into
 your lap. Then God tweaks the shawl
of Holy Moments you'd forgotten you were wearing. Then
 the world shouts
        the Word!
        round the flame of your heart.

Gyllian Davies

ANSWERING THE CALL

Several decades ago I dreamed of a primitive hand-axe that was hurtling toward me through time, crunching through the intervening civilizations. I was distressed to see that it was going to just pass me by, so I stepped over, into its path. Whatever it was bringing, I wanted to be the recipient. Now, all these years later, it makes sense.

For most of this time, I have followed a strong and steady impulse to research and reproduce the Stone Age sculptures of the Divine, which are overwhelmingly female. As much as we deny that God has any gender at all, we emphasize his maleness in pronouns and titles. Today there is no equivalent designation or respect for Goddess, should we feel the Divine to be female.

I began by collecting pictures of these remarkable figures, but I wanted to know them better. I wanted them in the round, at their real size. I sought out the few reproductions in existence, but my file of potent images was still barely tapped. I tried to convince my daughter, my niece and my friend, all sculptors, to make me more, but realized finally that I had to sculpt them myself.

I struggled to make them accurate in size and detail. It was hard to find pictures of their back sides. I bought many books and spent time on-line. Some of the early ones I've had to re-do as I got better skills and information.

And yet they came flowing out of me, in an order all their own. Sometimes they jostle each other to be next. Sometimes a brand new one will barge into line. Some must wait patiently for more information. All along, I've felt that I was the recipient, that they were taking the lead.

How strange for this little Quaker to be creating icons! I've had mystical experiences, enough to know that beyond this everyday reality there is something vast and awesome that is intimately connected to me, to each of us. I've also met a few awesome characters in dreams. And now these figures from long ago are demanding my attention. Both emotionally and logically I have to conclude that they are expressions of the Divine. Someone else's expressions, but with this urgency, they must also be mine.

Stone-Age Sculpture Collection   *by Kathy Hyzy*

Throughout this time I've been struggling with health issues. Almost three years ago I plummeted into a state that looked terminal, and indeed, the diagnosis I received was terminal. This dumped all plans and projects off my desk and left me open and empty to consider what I wanted to accomplish before I died. If only we could find this state of clarity voluntarily! If only we could orient our lives so thoroughly to our leadings!

My partner and I decided not to order a hospital bed, and instead set me up in my favorite recliner with a computer nearby and a little table full of drawers. I began to write my memoirs, to see if I could make larger sense out of my life. And I began to sculpt in earnest. Such an eagerness, a joy, sprang up with the sculpting! My mind grew quiet, my hands discovered a new wisdom and sureness. I felt a profound satisfaction. Here was the hand-axe of my dream.

What am I learning from these ancient women? The body, an older woman's body with all its lumps and bumps, is not ugly, is not an embarrassment, is not detached from Spirit, a drag on the Spirit, is not the concern or focus or possession of any man or nation. It is rather the core and essence of all life. It is the temple of new life and of the souls of the dead. It flows with milk and nourishment throughout life. It is deep and wise and mysterious. It is The Source.

Each of these figures is unique and carries a unique attitude. I found my own body echoing it – rising up in serene dignity or cavorting playfully. When I could take on this attitude, become inhabited by it, then I could express it in clay from my own soul. It became mine.

I've run into plenty of inaccurate reproductions that have been "improved upon" to the degree that they seem to have lost their potency. They seem romanticized. The frightening or baffling has been glossed over. Hands are more beneficent, faces less fierce. I didn't want to add my own paltry "wisdom," I wanted to be taken to brand new insights from this distant and mysterious time.

Within me were two monsters I had to tame: the bundle of modern assumptions I carry, and the capturing of an alien form and style. My first expression in clay was always an exaggeration, a subtle caricature that I had to tone down. It also often carried mysterious problems. One lion-person defied all my attempts until I realized I was making a person in lion costume, assuming a shaman. In reality, the back was longer, the legs shorter, the neck at an odd angle—what I was looking at was a lion standing on its hind legs, not a person at all. Discovering how strong my assumptions are is a very humbling experience.

I'm especially moved by the abstracted female forms. In art, any variation from the literal is a communication. My daughter made a sculpture of a huddled man with one arm reaching out. That arm is six or eight inches longer than reality. It carries all the aching plea for connection in those six or eight inches. That's where the emotional message lies. Over and over in the Stone Age, female figures appear that are reduced to an essence. Everything is stripped away except the one important message.

In art, any variation from the literal is a communication.

But ah, what is that message? That's as hard to define in words as a mystical experience. We don't have their stories, yet something within recognizes and resonates.

These images are archetypal, and lie deep within like rhizomes which give forth flowers true to the root year after year. The flower of the Paleolithic looks a lot like the flower that now blossoms in my dreams. After thousands of years of neglect and worse, the archetypal feminine is rising up, in me and in many others, men and women. This is not the feminine so carefully crafted by the patriarchs, this one is out of their control. She comes with a storm of righteous indignation and a bottomless heart of love for her suffering children.

I worked on a piece called the Mistress of the Animals (MOTA) from Hacilar in Anatolia. She is naked and well padded, and sits on a leopard, holding a leopard cub to her chest. She's very complex and took a month to do. I sculpted ten separate parts, hoping they were all accurate enough in scale they would fit together.

During this process, I had several big dreams where I seemed to be "channeling" the MOTA. In the first I watched a male eagle bring food to its three young in the nest. He fed the two nearest but neglected the third. This one, who became a mixture of bird and boy, began to whine and mutter complaints. I told him he could always leave if he didn't like it. Then I was by the nest, picking him up to carry him off. The father eagle looked at me, outraged. He turned upside down to watch me pass. I paused and said to him, "Oh, you want him? Then take better care of him!" I plunked the bird-boy onto his breast.

Mistress of the Animals, Hacilar by Lynn Waddington

To be the equal of the royal eagle, I was more than myself. I carried the MOTA, or rather, it was really the MOTA at work there within me. The eagle, symbol of American imperialism, is ripe for eldering, and that regal MOTA was more than a match for it.

It was only about a week later that I had another MOTA dream. This time, I came across two men, one mercilessly bullying the other. He ripped insignia off the other's uniform, laughed and waved it in the man's face. The other man was furious, clearly about to blow. I walked right up to them, pulled the victim aside, patted his chest and told him to take a few deep breaths. Then I turned to the bully, pulled him into my face by his shirt front, and said fiercely, "Don't you know, people get killed for this!" He immediately dropped the superior stance, looked at his shoes and said, "I know."

He seemed to just need a little help to get out of his old pattern. I think he also appreciated that I didn't condemn him, but rather was worried for him. Once again, the spirit of the Mother was addressing the ills of our modern world in her unique way, with concern for everyone. It felt astonishing to have that spirit expressed through me. I have a new appreciation for the men and women who are doing the work of non-violent conflict resolution and so many other forms of the great transformation. The feminine Spirit is freeing men as well as women to a life of creativity, compassion and justice.

Soon after, I dreamed that I sent my sculptures down into the depths to acquire their soul or spirit. The first was just coming back. I was astounded to see that it had been transformed into a radiant green leaf, bursting with life and energy. I was on my way to a seminar, where I was part of an experiment with jungle leaves. Climbing a long flight of stairs winded me enough to check my oxygen hose and discover that it wasn't attached to anything.

A young friend offered to go back down the stairs and hook me up. Instead of an oxygen machine, she found a supply of huge jungle leaves, but they were all dead and brown. I thought, oh well, in every experiment some receive the duds or placebos, and I guess that's just my fate this time. But then she found one last leaf that was glowing with health and life. When she hooked me up to it I felt its energy surge through me.

During the entire time of sculpting and writing, I was either improving or holding steady, both remarkable in a disease that knows only decline. For various reasons, I've stopped both activities for a few months now. During this time, my condition has been worsening, enough now to worry me. Only recently have I thought to connect the two, through writing this and through insightful comments from friends.

It's enough to make me seriously consider just how important it must be to pay attention to my Inner Guide, and to follow the promptings, whether I understand them or not. To follow them *now*, not at some later, more convenient time. These images must come forth. I must hook up to that glowing leaf that is my sculpture's newfound soul. It appears that this is not optional. It appears that this is a matter of life and death.

Lynn Waddington

The Buddhist monk Thich Nhat Hanh has said that "everything is linked to the presence of God at every moment." The practice of contemplative photography has helped me experience the truth of this statement within my daily life. In the practice, I look at familiar objects as if I've never seen them before, focusing on their colour, pattern and even texture. Whenever I do this, I notice many things I would normally pass by. In fact, the practice is most powerful when I view things that I would usually ignore. Sometimes even the most ordinary object or situation transforms into a dazzling display.

I have found that the practice of contemplative photography has some similarity to the unfolding that can occur in Silent Meeting. In Silent Meeting there is an initial period of settling my mind so that I can be receptive to hear that still small voice within and, should I feel called to speak, entering a process of quiet discernment before passing on the inner experience through spoken word.

Like in Silent Meeting, being receptive is the first phase in contemplative photography. Sometimes it can take a while to make the shift from 'looking for' an image to 'receiving' one that comes to me. Once something comes to my attention, the practice also requires that I enter into a process of discernment. Discernment involves engaging in an inner dialogue to become fully conscious of the distinct qualities that have come to my attention. For example, I might ask myself what exactly caught my eye. Was it the contrast of shadow and light or a particular pattern on part of an object?

The final stage of the practice is to photograph only those qualities that caught my eye and nothing more. The result is that often an image looks abstract – as the focal point may be a juxtaposition of colours, a repeating pattern or simply the play of light and shadow. And if the practice holds true through to the final phase, something of the quality of the initial encounter will be conveyed to the viewer of the image.

Whenever I notice something in this contemplative way, there is a surprising sense of intimacy, as if I am bearing witness to whatever has caught my attention. And in return I feel a sense of rejuvenation and delight. I have also noticed that my relationship with whatever I

While Slicing an Onion   *Sharon Driscoll*

have photographed is forever changed from one of disregard to one of appreciation and sometimes even awe. I began to wonder exactly what is it that I encounter in these moments.

George Fox advised that one should "walk softly upon the earth answering to that of God in everyone." I have always loved that statement because it presupposes that if we listen, we can hear God speaking in everyone. I wondered if Fox's statement could be extended to include not just everyone but everything. Were these moments a chance to know that of God within my ordinary surroundings? Was it God's presence in these moments which rejuvenated me and sometimes filled me with awe? Could making a photograph be my way of "answering" that of God's presence in whatever I encountered?

Probably the most important gift of this practice has nothing to do with photography. The gift is the confidence that at any moment I can soften my gaze and open to the sometimes amazing displays that lie in the periphery of my awareness. And in that moment it may be possible, as Thich Nhat Hanh has suggested, to link with the presence of God... in everything.

Sharon Driscoll

Quakers do not break the silence of Meeting for Worship casually. When the urge to speak can no longer be denied, a Friend stands, heart pounding and palms damp, to raise her voice in the silence. The force that moves Friends to vocal ministry is, I think, the same prompting of the soul that stimulates any kind of creative work. A trembling within, a passion to communicate urges us until we cannot refrain from speaking out, putting hands to keyboard, chisel to stone, voice to song, body to dance, paint to canvas.

My summons began with a badger.

Richard and I were driving home late one summer night after seeing Molly off at the airport when the glare of our truck headlights picked out a humped form on the pavement. I

The force that moves Friends to vocal ministry is, I think, the same prompting of the soul that stimulates any kind of creative work.

caught a glimpse of long-clawed feet, a broad back, and a white stripe bisecting a wide head as we rushed past.

"Badger!"

"Should I go back?" asked Richard.

We were both tired. But the image of that motionless shape on the pavement tugged my heart.

"Yes—please?"

He made a screaming U-turn in the two-lane highway, and drove back. I hopped out, darted across the dark road, and cautiously laid a hand on the still form. The fur was warm and the body unmarred —the animal might have been asleep— but not a muscle twitched. The badger was dead. My ears tuned for approaching traffic, I slid my hands under the limp body and then hefted it with a grunt, surprised at its solid weight.

"Do you need help?" Richard called from the truck.

"No," I said, a little out of breath.

I toted the badger off the pavement, climbed down the bank below the road and walked a few yards into the darkness of the desert. When I came to a large creosote bush, I knelt and slid the body from my arms to the earth. I sat for a moment reciting a silent prayer, one finger touching the badger's dense fur. Then I brushed my hands on my jeans, trotted back across the highway, and climbed into the waiting truck.

Richard reached over and gripped my hand. We drove away into the night.

After that, I started picking up roadkill: jackrabbits, pocket gophers, coyotes, rattlesnakes, deer, and turtles. The huge porcupine, armed with a profusion of golden quills. The great-horned owl, one wing still flapping in the backwash of passing vehicles. The soft plumage of the curve-billed thrasher: its yellow eye bright, its neck broken. I touched animals that, if alive, would never have allowed my approach. My hands remember the feel of their bodies, so like mine in the stitching of muscle to bone, yet so fundamentally different.

I didn't always stop. Sometimes I didn't have time or there was too much traffic. And I felt guilty as I drove on, the form on the pavement burned in my vision.

Richard got used to my habit. He's the one who put a folding shovel in the back of the truck, who made me wear gloves if the body was mangled or bloody, who hugged me afterwards.

When people asked why I stopped, I told them that I pulled roadkill off the pavement because I hated the waste. I quoted a biologist colleague: "If you get the bodies out of harm's way, they can decompose, and the critters that feed on them don't get killed too."

It's a matter of economy, I said, like never throwing away food. Moving roadkill off the highway allows the cycle of life to continue unbroken. The materials that make up one existence can recycle into others. It was a good speech: the scientist in me was pleased. But my heart knew there was more. I didn't trust that sense, and anyway, I couldn't find words for what I felt. I kept seeing the badger: its fur sleek, its muscles solid, its body as peaceful as if in sleep—but dead.

I come from a culture that trusts the logical conclusions of science without question. Science has much to say about the community of the land and the interrelationships that define and sustain that community, as well as about our place in it. Ecology seems to me among of the most reverential of the sciences. It honors all of life by listening to every voice without exception, giving words to creatures large and small, common and obscure — even those lying broken on the pavement. It chronicles the relationships that tell the great story of life as it flexes and fluctuates in its eternal dance with change, and the everyday miracle of reincarnation as the molecules from one being cycle through others from birth to death to birth, time and again. It is not the role of ecology to look for miracles or report on matters of heart and spirit. Still, reading between the lines of its data and theories, what shines out of the careful words is the presence of the sacred, demonstrated in the continuing rhythm of life as it makes a place for all of us on this green and animate planet.

What my heart reads in the lives I haul off the highway is a parallel we have either forgotten or that we ignore: How we treat our fellow humans is directly related to, and perhaps determined by, how we treat other animals. Psychologists say that people who commit violent crimes are likely to have grown up abusing other species, setting cats afire, beating dogs, swerving to hit critters on the road. Empathy for other lives is not mere squeamishness or childish over-sensitivity: it is inseparable from our care for each other. A civilized society is created as much by our private, every-day acts as it is by the laws we pass and the contracts we sign. Our personal behavior sets the model for what we expect of others.

I stop to lift mangled and battered carcasses off the pavement, moving them carefully out of harm's way, in order that life might continue its journey. For me, picking up roadkill is an act of respect and compassion. And it brings a bittersweet and unexpected gift: each body that I gather up in death touches my life with its story and the magic of its existence.

Susan J. Tweit

AFTER THE STORM

C.J. Shane

CONTRIBUTOR BIOGRAPHIES

Margery Post Abbott has been released by Multnomah Meeting in Portland, Oregon, for a ministry of teaching and writing. Her newest book, *To Be Broken and Tender,* will be published by Friends Bulletin Corp. in 2010. Along with co-editing *Walk Worthy of Your Calling: Quakers and the Traveling Ministry*, with Peggy Parsons, Marge has two other books about Friends: *A Certain Kind of Perfection* and *The Historical Dictionary of the Friends (Quakers)*, as well as three Pendle Hill pamphlets.

Alicia Adams has lived in various states and in Puerto Rico, Venezuela, Canada and India. In 1974 she joined Victoria Friends Meeting, Victoria, British Columbia. She attended Meetings in Arizona and California, joining Berkeley Friends Meeting in 1990. She lives in Mimbres, New Mexico, with her partner, Daniel Richards; they attend Gila Friends Meeting. She's published articles in *Friends Journal, Western Friend* and *What Canst Thou Say*.

David H. Albert of Olympia Friends Meeting in Washington is a father, husband, author, magazine columnist, itinerant storyteller, and educator. He is clerk of his Meeting's Right Sharing of World Resources committee, and has been working for more than 30 years with a Gandhian land reform-related organization in South India (www.friendsoflafti.org) In his spare time, his hobby is rewriting the Old Testament. His website is www.skylarksings.com.

Beta Anderson has worn many hats. She has been an electrician, an organic farmer, a technical writer, a landlord, an artist, a fiddler, and now a Quaker. She and her partner, Barbara Leedy, attend Olympia Monthly Meeting. She is enjoying both the process and the silence.

Peter Anderson teaches writing at Adams State College in Alamosa, Colorado. Previously, he taught in the Ministry of Writing program at Earlham School of Religion. His collection of essays, *First Church of the Higher Elevations*, was published by Ghost Road Press in 2005. He lives on the western edge of the Sangre de Cristo Range and is a member of Durango Monthly Meeting.

Reza Antoszewska sometimes attends Multnomah Monthly Meeting in Portland, Oregon. She learned to make Ebru monprints from a Turkish Ebru master, Feridun Ozgoren. View more of her work online at fineartstudioonline.com/rezaantoszewska.

Maria Arrington became a convinced Friend in 1975 under the care of Gwynedd Meeting in Southeastern Pennsylvania. She moved to Northwestern Montana in 1989 and has worked there as a nurse ever since. At present she works in public health and has a private practice offering integrative healing techniques. She is a part of Glacier Valley Worship Group, under the care of Missoula Friends Meeting.

Kathy Barnhart is a member of Strawberry Creek Meeting in Berkeley, California, mostly retired from work as a psychotherapist and marriage counselor. She has two adult children, a husband and a one-eyed black cat, and enjoys photography, birding, cooking, reading and anything outdoors.

Heidi Blocher is a longtime Friend now sojourning with Phoenix Friends Meeting in Arizona. Her essay also appeared in the German publication *Quaeker*.

Cherrill Boissonou, a member of Corvallis Monthly Meeting, paints a wide variety of subjects, but says colors, shapes and even words provide the inspiration that makes her reach for a canvas and materials. She especially enjoys combining travel with painting utilizing pastels, ink and acrylics to capture her impressions. Cherrill is affiliated with Art in the Valley, a Corvallis art gallery. The corver artwork, "Shot Through", was inspired by a poem by 15th Century poet Kabir.

Helen Bruner is an attender at Berkeley Friends Meeting. She enjoys her practice of psychotherapy, a tapestry of classes in Bleak House, Playback Theater, Ericksonian Hypnotherapy and Dream Analysis, as well as friends, reading, writing and playing Scrabble. The last two years she's worked extensively with the Alternatives to Violence Project, which she re-discovered through a wonderful *Western Friend* article. "Fusion" was originally published in the Summer 2000 issue of *Poetalk*.

Charity Bryson has been a member of Grass Valley Friends Meeting in the beautiful Sierra Foothills of California for nearly twenty years, and has served on several committees there. She has been published in *Rattlesnake Review* (Sacramento) and has been a featured poet for their online publication. *Nevada County Poetry Series* included her poems in three of their yearly anthologies. She has received several awards from the local county fair.

Annette Carter is a member of Multnomah Meeting in Portland, Oregon. She teaches English as a Second Language and enjoys hiking and spending time with her family, especially her granddaughter.

Darlene Colborn is a member of Eugene Friends Meeting in Eugene, Oregon. Her poem "Living Peacefully" is a gift from her granddaughter.

Eleanor Dart is a lifelong Quaker. She resides in Tucson, Arizona, where she is a member of Pima Friends Meeting. Eleanor is a Licensed Professional Counselor. She now works on U.S. Army bases several times a year, counseling soldiers and the wives of soldiers. Often her assignments place her on bases in Germany, where in her father's footsteps, she seeks to bring help and comfort to those who suffer from war.

Gyllian Davies is a spirituality and creativity coach, certified spiritual director, art educator, artist and poet. She is also trained as a labyrinth and SoulCollage facilitator. A member of Bridge City Monthly Meeting in Portland, Oregon, her passion is taking people on a journey through the creative realm to discover the powerhouse of their own relationship with the Holy. To learn more check out www.TheHeartInfusedLife.com

Marian Wolfe Dixon is a regular attender at Multnomah Monthly Meeting in Portland, Oregon. A former Research Fellow with the Oregon Center for Complementary and Alternative Medicine, she is the author of three books on wellness: *Bodylessons* (2005), *Myofascial Massage* (2007) and *Body Mechanics and Self Care Manual* (2001). "Pain has been an awe inspiring teacher for me about strength and vulnerability, patience and well being", she says.

Sharon Driscoll has been a member of Berkeley Friends Meeting for more than twenty years. She currently lives in Nova Scotia with her husband, Sheldon Mitchell, but stays in touch with her home Meeting and visits Berkeley when she can. She has engaged in photography for many years and has a contemplative photography website called www.quieteyereflections.ca, which is named to honour Sylvia Shaw Judson's book *The Quiet Eye*.

Connie Fledderjohann is a member of Mendocino Monthly Meeting in California. Nature photography, especially macro photography, puts her in touch with the Great Mystery.

Iris Graville lives on Lopez Island in Washington, where she writes, does book arts, and attends the Lopez Island Worship Group. Her first book, *Hands at Work—Portraits and Profiles of People Who Work with Their Hands,* was published in 2009.

Robert Griswold is a member of Mountain View Friends Meeting in Denver, Colorado. In 1999-2000, he was the Brinton Visitor to Pacific Yearly Meeting. He has had articles, letters and book reviews published in *Friends Bulletin* (now *Western Friend*), *Friends Journal,* and *Quaker Theology*, plus two pamphlets, *Quaker Peace Testimony in Times of Terrorism* and *Creeds and Quakers: What's Belief Got To Do With It?* (Pendle Hill pamphlet #377).

Jami Hart is a member of Multnomah Monthly Meeting in Portland, Oregon.

Virginia Herrick is a member of Bellingham Friends Meeting in Western Washington. A freelance writer and editor, she has lived in the Pacific Northwest for nearly twenty years. Virginia lives with her husband, two children, three cats, dog, rabbit and rat, in a house next to a gigantic Grand fir tree. They enjoy lakes, bays, creeks, rivers, mountains and forests all around them, every day.

Phyllis Hoge of Albuquerque Meeting taught poetry in the University of Hawai'i English Department for twenty years, then retired from Honolulu to Albuquerque. In Hawai'i she raised three sons and one daughter, published five books of poetry, invented the first Poets in Schools program in the USA, and became a Quaker. She has traveled widely—Japan, China, Egypt, Mexico, Israel, Vietnam, Thailand, Senegal, Europe. Recent books: *The Painted Clock* and *Letters from JianHui.*

Susan Davis Hopkins is a part of Grass Valley Monthly Meeting in California. As a parent, grandparent and educator of young children, she has long been a storyteller, not usually in the oral tradition, but more often in visual and written forms. Quilts always tell stories. The fun of telling the Underground Railroad Story using the quilt as a medium was an exciting and joyful spiritual quest for her.

Betsey Kenworthy's experience of God was woven into her early life through nature, people and a church where there was music, dance, service, adventure and questioning. She was drawn to Quakers through Earlham College. In 1975, she and her husband sold their Alaskan home and sailed with two small sons for a year. It changed their lives. They've been part of Multnomah Meeting since 1978.

Eileen R. Kinch is a 2007 graduate of Earlham School of Religion, where she studied writing as ministry. Her book, *The ESR Story: 1985-2010*, was published in September 2009 in honor of the school's 50th anniversary. She is also the author of essays and poetry. A freelance writer and editor, Eileen lives in Lancaster County, Pennsylvania. She attends Keystone Fellowship Friends Meeting.

Shari Lane wandered by chance into the Reedwood Friends meeting in Portland, Oregon, hoping for guidance and comfort. Ken Comfort spoke, and she knew she had found a home. She holds degrees in Comparative Literature, Classics, and Law—an employment lawyer by day, writer by night. She is supported in both efforts by a generous husband, two (sometimes generous) children, and two wonderful but very hairy dogs.

Sara Lee lives in the Boise hinterlands, where she holds Silent Meeting for one in her home, or occasionally attends Boise Valley Friends Meeting. She was an attender at Boulder Friends Meeting for 15 years, and her grandmother Sara was Quaker. An educator working with migrant and Title I (poverty background) students, she has also produced Native American conference reports for FCNL.

Jeanne Lohmann has published eight collections of poetry and two volumes of prose. Her work appears in many journals and anthologies. She's been a member of the Religious Society of Friends for more than fifty years, in Chicago, Denver, San Francisco, and currently in Olympia, Washington. She has taught poetry classes at Pendle Hill and at Ben Lomond Quaker Center, and continues this vocation in Olympia.

Anthony Manousos—peace activist, writer, and teacher—serves on the board of directors for several interfaith organizations, including Interfaith Communities United for Justice and Peace. For twelve years he edited the Quaker magazine *Friends Bulletin* (now *Western Friend*) and edited four books and wrote several Quaker pamphlets. He has taught at Rutgers and Pepperdine, among other campuses, and currently resides in Culver City, California, where he is a member of Santa Monica Meeting.

Maria Melendez's collection of poetry, *How Long She'll Last in This World*, was a finalist for the 2007 PEN Center USA Literary Awards. Her next poetry collection, *Flexible Bones*, is forthcoming in 2010. A member of Logan Monthly Meeting in northern Utah, she currently lives in Pueblo, Colorado. In 2010 she will be the new editor of *Pilgrimage*, an independant literary magazine emphasizing spirit, witness and place.

Susan Merrill is a member of Olympia Friends Meeting in Olympia, Washington. She wrote "Mother Nature, My Mother and Me" while Clerk of North Branch Meeting in Wilkes-Barre, Pennsylvania. It was published in the Spring 1997 issue of *Friendly Woman*.

Mary Miche is a member of Strawberry Creek Meeting who attends Lake County Worship Group. She works with children as a therapist in local public schools, as a music educator in inner city Oakland and as the director of a summer program, Peace Camp. She also trains teachers through Fresno Pacific University. Much of her poetry was written during difficult life circumstances.

Markley Morris is an artist, filmmaker and long-time nonviolent activist. For more than seven years he shepherded the weekly Quaker vigil that began in October 2001 at the San Francisco Federal Building. He is a part of San Francisco Friends Meeting.

Peggy Senger Parsons is a Quaker Minister from Salem, Oregon, where she is the pastor of Freedom Friends Church (freedomfriends. org). She has traveled nationally and internationally preaching and teaching. She is a Licensed Professional Counselor with a specialty in trauma healing, and a certified spiritual director. Peggy writes regularly on topics of spirituality. You can find her blog and order books at sillypoorgospel.blogspot.com

Rob Pierson lives with his wife and two sons in Albuquerque, New Mexico, where he currently serves as the clerk of Oversight and Counsel for Albuquerque Monthly Meeting of the Religious Society of Friends. He trained as a geophysicist, works as a technologist, manager and engineer, and is currently in his third year of the Master of Ministry program at the Earlham School of Religion through the on-line Access program.

David Ray's recent books include *When* (Howling Dog Press) and *After Tagore: Poems Inspired by Rabindranath Tagore* (Nirala Editions). *Music of Time: Selected & New Poems* (Backwaters Press) offers work from fifteen previous volumes. Other titles include *The Death of Sardanapalus* and *Other Poems of the Iraq Wars* (from which "Out of the Silence", included here, is reprinted) and a memoir, *The Endless Search*. David is a member of Pima Monthly Meeting in Tucson. Visit www.

davidraypoet.com to learn more.

Judy Ray's most recent book is *To Fly Without Wings: Poems* (Helicon Nine Editions, 2009). Recent chapbooks include *Fishing in Green Waters, Sleeping in the Larder: Poems of a Sussex Childhood,* and *Judy Ray: Greatest Hits 1974–2008.* In Tucson, Judy spends some of her time as a volunteer teacher of English as a Second Language to adults in the community. She is an active member of Pima Monthly Meeting.

Trudy Myrrh Reagan, born in 1936, is a professional artist (www. myrrh-art.com.) She grew up in East Tennessee, attended Westtown Friends School and many workcamps, then Stanford. The civil rights and sanctuary movements influenced her life. She is a member of Palo Alto Friends Meeting and facilitates its projects in El Salvador. As an artist in Silicon Valley who has a physicst husband, she founded YLEM: Artists Using Science and Technology.

Eric E. Sabelman, PhD, is a biomedical engineer in the Kaiser Permanente Neurosurgery Department in Redwood City, California, treating Parkinson's Disease. He first attended Quaker meeting in Pasadena in 1969, and became a member of Palo Alto Friends Meeting about 20 years later. He is currently clerk of College Park Quarterly Meeting. He and his wife, Mary Ann, have two grown children and live in Menlo Park, California.

C.J. Shane is a member of Pima Friends Meeting, in Tucson, Arizona. She is a graduate of the University of Texas at Austin and the University of Kentucky at Lexington. Shane is a painter, printmaker, and creator of artist's books (www.cjshane.com). The natural world, especially the beautiful Sonoran Desert, is the greatest source of grounding and inspiration in her life and work.

Don Elton Smith is a member of Fort Collins Friends Meeting in Fort Collins, Colorado. He has been a Friend for more than 55 years, and he and his wife Harriet helped start Meetings in both Grass Valley, California and the Monterey Peninsula. He lives in Loveland, Colorado.

D. Pablo Stanfield joined University Monthly Meeting (Seattle) in 1983. Quaker service includes Friends World Committee for Consulatation and Monroe Friends Worship Group in the Washington State Reformatory. A lead trainer in the Alternatives to Violence Project, he volunteered over 22 years in prisons. A translator of Quaker literature into Spanish, he's traveled with Peace Brigades International (Central America). His writing appears in *Relentless*

Persistence: Nonviolent Action in Latin America.

cubbie storm is a newish Quaker. He grew up in Florida and Wisconsin, has lived in Washington State and now makes his home in Berkeley, California. He is a member of San Francisco Monthly Meeting. His blog is *seams of a peculiar queer* at peculiarqueer. wordpress.com.

Biliana Stremska grew up an atheist in the anti-religious culture of Communist Bulgaria before the collapse of the Berlin Wall (1970's-1980's). She is a member of Berkeley Friends Meeting in California.

Tina Tau is a member of Multnomah Monthly Meeting in Portland, Oregon. She teaches Humanities in a Montessori middle school in Portland. She is currently working on a book about using dreams for spiritual guidance. Her poetry has been published in *Friends Journal, Calyx, Wilderness* and other journals.

Susan Tweit is a member of Las Cruces Meeting in New Mexico, but lives in South-central Colorado. She is a scientist who studied grizzly bear habitat, wildfire patterns, and sagebrush communities until she realized that she loved telling the stories in the data more than collecting those data. She has authored a dozen books and hundreds of articles exploring the relationships that make up the community of nature--our own species included. "Picking Up Roadkill" is an excerpt from *Walking Nature Home*, University of Texas Press, 2009.

Lynn Waddington is a member of University Friends Meeting in Seattle, Washington, and attends Whidbey Island Worship Group. She also produced a video about what she learned through her call to sculpt these prehistoric images of the feminine divine, titled *When God was Female.*

Ashley M. Wilcox is a member of Freedom Friends Church in Salem, Oregon, and a sojourning member of University Friends Meeting in Seattle, Washington. She blogs at questforadequacy.blogspot.com.

Nancy Wood lives in Santa Cruz, California. She and her husband have been married for 20 years and have two children. Nancy is a member of Santa Cruz Monthly Meeting. She grew up in a Quaker family and attended a Friends School. Her fiction has been published online, in *Long Story Short* and *Tuesday Shorts*.

Order these other titles from us online at WesternFriend.org

Compassionate Listening
and Other Writings by Gene Knudsen Hoffman

edited by Anthony Manousos

Quaker Gene Knudsen Hoffman dedicated much of her life to seeking out the deep, psychological causes of violence and to helping bring about healing and reconciliation through a process she calls "Compassionate Listening." Her work inspired Leah Green to begin The Compassionate Listening Project, whose workshops have taught hundreds of people how to listen with their hearts and well as minds. This collection of writings sheds light on Hoffman's life and inspiration.

EarthLight: Spiritual Wisdom for an Ecological Age

edited by Cindy Spring and Anthony Manousos

During its fifteen years of publication, *EarthLight* magazine celebrated the living Earth and our thirteen billion year story of the universe. Founded and inspired by Quakers, *EarthLight* featured articles by the world's seminal figures in secular and religious thought about the place and participation of humankind in creation. This anthology embodies the best of *EarthLight* and of Quaker writers on spirituality and ecology during the past twenty years. Contributors include Maya Angelou, Thomas Berry, Jim Corbett, Joanna Macy, Terry Tempest Williams and many others.

Western Quaker Reader: Writings by and About Independent
Quakers in the Western US, 1929-1999

edited by Anthony Manousos

This collection provides vivid, first-person testimonies by Friends involved in the "reinvention" of Quakerism in the Western USA from the 1930's to the present. This is the first historical work about Western Quakerism written from the viewpoint of Independent Friends, and the only one that describes the development of Intermountain and North Pacific Yearly Meetings—some of the most vital, lively Yearly Meetings in the USA today.

LaVergne, TN USA
25 March 2010
177200LV00004B/126/P